THE LEARNING SPECTRUM
IN
CHILD DEVELOPMENT

I0023533

Developmental Psychology
in
Marie Montessori
Jean Piaget
Erik Erikson

By John H. Morgan, Ph.D., D.Sc., Psy.D.

John H. Morgan

THE LEARNING SPECTRUM IN CHILD DEVELOPMENT

Developmental Psychology
in

Marie Montessori
Jean Piaget
Erik Erikson

By John H. Morgan
Ph.D.(Hartford), D.Sc.(London), Psy.D. (FH/Oxford)
978-155605-493-8 P
978-155605-494-5 E
Copyright © 2021 John H. Morgan

Wyndham Hall Press
Levering, MI

INTRODUCTION

In its fledgling state of development, this branch of psychology focused almost exclusively upon issues related to the developmental learning in infancy and early childhood. Subsequent development under the leadership of key figures in the field of education such as Marie Montessori, Jean Piaget, and Erik Erikson saw developmental psychology as it came to be called evolve into one of the most active and vital sub-specializations within psychology. Under the leadership of Karen Horney, Melanie Klein, and Anna Freud, psychopathology moved into the field of child development and created a whole new area of specialization in clinical psychotherapy as I have explored in my 2019 book, *Child Psychopathology in Clinical Practice*. In the following study, we will concentrate our attention upon child development and stay within the confines of developmental psychology as it has come to be known and defined. Though our interest here will be upon the learning spectrum of child development demonstrated in the pioneering work of Montessori, Piaget, and Erikson, we will begin with a general overview and introduction of the broad field of developmental psychology itself before focusing our attention upon the learning spectrum as explored by our three pioneers.

Naturally and understandably, many would wish to add names to the list of distinguished scholars and researchers in the field of child developmental psychology and learning theory but no one in the relevant fields of study would question the central importance of Montessori, Piaget, and Erikson. In the following, we will take a close look at each of these creative pioneers in terms of their own personal life story as well as the key contributions to theory and practice in fields relevant to the learning spectrum in child development. A close look at the emergence of what Montessori chose to call "scientific pedagogy" will lead to an inquiry into Piaget's "genetic epistemology" concluding with a careful assessment of Erikson's "stages of development" in the life cycle all with an eye towards a better understanding of the appearance of developmental psychology in the 20th century and its relevance to learning theory and cognitive development of children today.

Chapter One

What is Developmental Psychology?

Developmental psychology is the study of the lifespan of humans from birth to death and focuses its attention upon the how and why of measurably identifiable change that occurs over time. Though once concentrating on issues related to infant and early childhood development, in today's world of psychological research, the field has aggressively moved to include the full spectrum of the maturation process from infancy and childhood through adolescence to old age. Research interests center its attention upon such processes as thinking, feeling, and the behavioral changes which occur through life including particularly three fundamental dimensions, viz., physical, cognitive, and socio-emotional development. These fundamental categories of research and study will cover a broad spectrum of topics including motor skills, executive functions, moral understanding, language acquisition, the phenomenon of social change, personality development and variations including the inevitable emotional development and aberrations, the dynamics of the self-concept, and necessarily identity formation of the individual from infancy through time into adulthood and old age. Though our interest in the following study will be upon the learning spectrum in child development, we will continually be reminded of the importance of anticipating the eventuality of old age and geriatric issues related to emotional well-being as I have explored in my 2018 book, *Geriatric Psychotherapy*.

Early on a leading topic in the developing field focused upon the relationship of nature to nurture in the process of human development both in terms of existential context as well as over time. Though continuing controversy and conflicting positions occur within the research community, there is a general understanding that issues related to individual behavioral matrices, socio-cultural and physical environmental factors all constitute a legitimate focus of research attention taking full account of both the biological and neurological components of all stages of physical and emotional development within the individual. The exponential acceleration of the scope of developmental psychology from its early days is suggestive of the vitality of research opportunities available in this burgeoning field of psychology including sub-sets such as specifically educational psychology, child psychopathology as well as child psychoanalysis, various forms of forensic psychology and child development psychology with continuing and accelerating dimensions of cognitive, ecological, and cultural psychology as relates to child development.

Names which are most commonly associated with developmental psychology include Urie Bronfenbrenner, Erik Erikson, Sigmund Freud, Jean Piaget, Barbara Rogoff, Esther Thelen, Lev Vygotsky, Karen Horney, and Melanie Klein. However, in this study we will focus upon Erikson and Piaget as highly recognized as authorities in the field as well as Marie Montessori who has too often and quite unjustifiably been overlooked, discounted, or disregarded owing to her heavily pedagogically focused praxis orientation in this field. At the end of the day as we will suggest, it is insufficient to have developed refined theories in developmental psychology without having demonstrated their effectiveness and, therefore, the justification for including Montessori in our discussion of Erikson and Piaget who themselves were theoretically motivated applied researchers.

   To have a deeper appreciation for the appearance and now indispensable relevance of developmental psychology, it will be of some value to track the historical emergence and expansive cultivation of this field of study realizing, of course, that much of the impetus for the development of this field traces its beginnings back to the early days of behaviorism and the work of John B. Watson (1878-1958) and the influence Jean-Jacques Rousseau (1644-1699) had in its formative stage.   Rousseau, well before Watson, identified three stages of development in his now recognized classic book, *Emile: Or, On Education*, which were infancy, childhood, and adolescence, categories which still today dominant the discussion.   From its inception, the points of interest had to do with the how and why of changes in the individual over time from infancy through adulthood affecting cognitive, social, intellectual, and personality features of an individual's life span.   We will later, for example, investigate carefully the eight stages of psychological development introduced by Erik Erikson based on his study with Montessori and Anna Freud wherein he demonstrated that there is a developmental process throughout the life of an individual, from infancy to old age, which can be identified and cultivated for the improvement of the quality of life of the individual.   The influence of Sigmund Freud and the psychoanalytic theories of personality development were not inconsequential in this regard.   Watson, Erikson, and Freud as well as most psychologists of the early/mid-20th century have been greatly influenced by the evolutionary theories of Charles Darwin whose work suggested the central importance of developmental understanding of the human species (including our emotional life) such that the first President of the American Psychological Association, G. Stanley Hall, aggressively promoted the study of childhood development in learning. His influence was particularly reflected in the published works of James Mark Baldwin, author of *Imitation: A Chapter in the Natural History of Consciousness* and *Mental Development in the Child and the Race: Methods and Processes*.

Rather than singular monolithic theory of psychological development, there is a plethora of theories and systems embodying those theories applied to a full range of research areas. Here we will simply review very briefly a listing of the more popular systems and not particularly in chronological order, but clearly we must begin with Freud's psychosexual developmental theory as it was the earliest fully developed system and has had a tremendous influence in the overall research of developmental psychology as a fully developed school of thought within psychology. Freud's three tiered theory of the human psyche being comprised of the conscious, preconscious, and unconscious strata, personality development must be linked to this operative model of maturation from self-awareness, recollection and memory, and repressed materials affecting behavior.

The tension between self-awareness (consciousness) and psychic repression (unconscious materials) can result in the development of anxiety and neurosis and, therefore, the development of an emotionally healthy person is dependent upon the careful management of the tripartite composition of personality structure, i.e., the id, the ego, and the superego. The healthy development of personality symmetry requires the pleasure-seeking id and the moralizing super-ego to be managed towards a successful navigation of reasonable and acceptable patterns of behavior. Because Freud's five stages of development were the first and continue to have a profound influence on the furtherance of stage-development theories in human maturation, it seems fitting that they at least be briefly defined here.

Psychoanalytic theory requires there to be a linking of the maturation process with erogenous zones of the body relevant in the psychosexual manifestations of the developmental process. The oral stage, being the first, covers the time period from birth to about one year during which stage the libido of the infant is localized in the mouth. The second stage covers from one to three years and is anal in locality and constitutes a preoccupation of the young child's attention to bodily functions. From three to five years of age during which time the fundamentals of the child's personality are being formed, there is an awareness of and acute attention paid to the phallic stage relative to the child's genitalia and secondary sexual organs. The fourth stage constitutes the period of latency from age five to the onset of puberty and is characterized by a growing repression of sexual interest followed by the fifth and final stage of genitalia coming during puberty and lasting throughout adulthood. Clearly, from a psychoanalytic perspective, these five stages of maturation are crucial in understanding the development of the human psyche and constitute the matrices within which mental health as well as mental illness occurs.

Though little has been written or said about the congruency of Piaget's theory of cognitive development in the child learning process with Maria Montessori's approach to pedagogical techniques, clearly there is a connection of some significance and merit which will be subsequently dealt with in this book. Jean Piaget (1896-1980) is considered one of the leading child psychologists working in the field of learning and pedagogical theory of cognitive development. His overriding theory, as we will discuss in detail later in Chapter Three, was that there is a direct relationship between the child's involvement with the learning process through practical praxis-based hands-on experience and encounter with new materials being presented. Rather than simply reciting information learned through rote instruction, the child learns through an existential involvement with the information materials themselves thereby constituting a constructionist posture to the newly introduced materials, that is, the child actually engages in the construction of a system of insight and knowledge based on the experiential encounter itself through an incrementally developing sequence and arrangement of that new materials such that it makes sense to the child. Piaget proposed four stages in this developmental construction and not necessarily at any particularly designated age, i.e., sensorimotor, pre-operational, concrete operational, and formal operational. These will be delineated and discussed in some detail in Chapter Three.

One of the abiding concerns among child psychologists is the development of a theory of moral development, a concern which occupied Piaget himself and many of the leading theorists of the day including Karen Horney, Melanie Klein, and Anna Freud but particularly Maria Montessori and Erik Erikson under the leadership of Piaget and his colleagues. One of those colleagues was Lawrence Kohlberg (1927-1987). His work consisted fundamentally of an expansion of Piaget's contention, based on clinical evidence gleaned over many years of study, that the logic of moral development occurs through the constructive process of maturation in the child's cognitive reflectivity.

Kohlberg believed, based on his own extension of Piaget's clinical studies, that it is the concept of justice itself which is the driving factor in moral development beginning in the child but progressing throughout life. In his systemic analysis of the developmental processes operative within the moral sensibilities of the maturing child, Kohlberg suggested three distinct levels of moral reasoning within the child, i.e., pre-conventional moral reasoning, conventional moral reasoning, and post-conventional moral reasoning. Pre-conventional moral reasoning is most common among children wherein the rational process of assessment has to do with the primacy of rewards and punishments related to a matrix of behavior which results in either being rewarded or punished depending on the chosen action. The second level of moral reasoning, i.e., conventional moral reasoning, begins to appear in later childhood and early adolescence in which the decisions made regarding behavior are based upon a reasonable understanding of the rules and guidelines made by society at large whereas the third and final level of moral reasoning called post-conventional, is suggestive of the individual whose maturation has led to an understanding that the rules and guidelines of society generally are not solid and objective but relative and subjective and that authority itself is subject to rationalization. Kohlberg's favorite illustration of his developmental levels of moral reasoning was what is classically known as the Heinz Dilemma in which the husband of a wife dying from cancer was faced with the dilemma of whether or not to steal the needed drug for which he could not actually afford.

In Chapter Four we will delineate with discussion the full scope of the psychosocial developmental theory of Erik Erikson (1902-1994) but for purposes of presenting the several currently operative models of developmental psychology, it seems appropriate here to briefly present his system of thought developed, it should be pointed out, in collaboration with his wife Joan Erikson. Now famously touted as a dominant analytical construct, the Eriksons developed over a number of years based on their own clinical research eight stages of psychosocial development through which individuals must pass from infancy through to old age if they are to experience good emotional health and well-being. Each of the stages has been given a descriptive name as well as a sequential number and the Eriksons were keen to place what they called a "virtue" or a value upon the positive side of each developmental stage. The first stage is that of "Trust versus Mistrust," which occurs during infancy and the sought for virtue is that of hope in which the infant learns who can be trusted with hopeful confidence that they will always be there for the infant. The second stage is called "Autonomy versus Shame and Doubt" with the primary virtue being that of the will during which time the maturing child explores the range of possible independence based on their own capacities for expressiveness within the context of the authoritative figure in their supervision which either allows for greater freedom facilitating confidence or greater supervision which can foster low self-esteem and doubt. The experience is essentially a testing of the will of the maturing child within the matrix of care and protection.

At a time in the child's life when playmates become increasingly important in the maturation process of socialization, the third stage of development is called "Initiative versus Guilt" with the presenting virtue is that of perceived purpose within the matrix of playing with peers and siblings. Characterized by curiosity and inquisitiveness within the context of play, the child will engage in incessant questioning within the context of this curious drive to know and understand, such that if the child's initiative is encouraged and rewarded there will be healthy growth towards maturity. If, on the other hand, it is discouraged or disparaged, there is the danger of a deep-seated feeling of guilt stifling development creating present and long-term difficulties in communicating with peers and authority figures.

The cultivation of a sense of accomplishment and basic functional competency as the child enters school age constitutes the basic virtue of the fourth stage of development, namely, "Industry versus Inferiority." Industry in this nomenclature implies competency of intentionality in functional behavior in which the child strives for acknowledgment and for the affirmation of his peers and classmates such that fitting in and becoming one of the group becomes a driving force in the child's efforts for approval and the avoidance of rejection and failure which fosters feelings of inferiority. The virtue of loyalty and belonging is called fidelity by Erikson and characterizes the fifth stage of development consisting of "Identity versus Role Confusion." In adolescence, the individual is feeling the pressures and attractions of becoming his/her own person within the social matrix of their world and learning what it means to be a part of a group, an individual with a personal identity within the framework of a social matrix including very importantly an identify with their own sense of gender becomes crucial in avoiding anxiety and uncertainty about fitting into a niche of pleasure and satisfaction.

Gender identity which has occurred in stage five now takes on a significant role in early adulthood where the individual is being motivated to seek out opportunities for emotional attachments so that the sixth stage of development is classified as "Intimacy versus Isolation," suggesting that if the individual is successful in his/her search for intimacy and emotional attachment then the ever impending danger of isolation and loneliness has been avoided for ultimately love is the virtue of this stage in life. If and when the individual is successful in avoiding loneliness and finding deeply abiding emotional attachments, the seventh stage of

"Generativity versus Stagnation" provides a real opportunity for settling down with a drive towards self-care as a defining virtue of this stage in maturing adulthood. This time period provides an opportunity for the creating of a family life and community involvement lest one drift off into tepidity and a life devoid of ambition. The final stage in life according to this Eriksonian model is "Ego Integrity versus Despair" with a strong sense of maturity and wisdom as the accompanying virtue of reaching old age. The inclination to look back upon one's passing life is natural and one does it with satisfaction and contentment or with a sense of failure and lost opportunity. Contentment or despair constitutes the choices in later life as one assesses from whence one has come in anticipation of one's inevitable decline and demise.

On the heels of this Eriksonian model of psychosocial development comes the work of Michael Commons who has developed what is recognized as a model of hierarchical complexity (MHC) with his intentions being to modify Piaget's development system but not based on what is essentially domain-specific information but rather task-based ordering of performance behavior. For Commons, a development stage is suggestive of the ordering of the complexity of a behavioral matrix into a hierarchical arrangement which is successively and successfully completed or accomplished. Not satisfied with only eight stages of development as purported by Piaget, Commons proceeded to expand the roster to include some sixteen stages which we will list here as 0 Calculatory; 1 Sensory & Motor; 2 Circular sensory-motor; 3 Sensory-motor; 4 Nominal; 5 Sentential; 6 Preoperational; 7 Primary; 8 Concrete; 9 Abstract; 10 Formal; 11 Systematic; 12 Metasystematic; 13 Paradigmatic; 14 Cross-paradigmatic; 15 Meta-Cross-paradigmatic. These are all based on a calculation relative to the difficulty of accomplishment and ranked in a hierarchy of sequence. Within the scope of the definitional time parameters of each stage, there are essentially three fundamental rules for their ordering in a logical sequence from less difficult to more difficult or less refined to more refined thereby creating a hierarchy of functionality (one cannot help but be reminded of Maslow's Hierarchy of Needs).

Though poorly named in translation as the ecological systems theory of psychological development (EST), the Russian psychologist Urie Bronfenbrenner (1917-2005) created an analytical mechanism of developmental analysis built around the psycho-social environment within which individuals actually are born into and live throughout their lives, moving from one environment to another. He devised four systems of analysis, viz., microsystem, mesosystem, exosystem, and macrosystem, each embodying its own set of rules which profoundly affect the formative development of the individual and are constructed in such a fashion as to suggest incremental development over time. For example, the microsystem is oriented around home and school whereas the mesosystem has to do with the developmental features of interpersonal relationships created and nurtured in the micro world of home and school. The exosystem constitutes the much larger matrix of social interaction of the larger society within which the individual is situated into adulthood and the macrosystem clearly incorporates the full spectrum of culture and society, the *weltanschauung* or ethos of the individual's interactive personal world of relationships. From its inception shared in Bronfenbrenner's 1979 book titled *The Ecology of Human Development,* this analytical system has gained much international attention and a tremendous following among developmental psychologists such that this system of thought is considered a central component of all life studies today.

Two more systems of developmental psychology deserve at least a mention before we move into a deeper exploration of this field and they are what are labeled "evolutionary developmental psychology" (EDP) and "attachment theory" (AT) developed by John Bowlby. Evolutionary development theory is a research paradigm built upon the Darwinian principle of evolutionary development in which natural selection plays a major part in understanding the developmental process of human behavior and of cognitive capabilities. EDP consists of both a careful consideration of the significance of genetics and the environmental factors which undergird the social and cognitive capabilities of the human person including what Piaget has identified as the gene-environment interactions called epigenetics modulating these various processes to the actual learning and living environment of the individual. Environmental variety constitutes a major factor in developmental trajectory of the individual rather than merely a one-directional pattern of development based on the domain assumption that natural selection itself when operationally connected to developmental choices becomes a key factor in the symmetry and balance of the individual's personalized development progression sometimes called "adaptive developmental plasticity."

It was the British psychologist John Bowlby (1907-1990) who elevated the conversation about personal development with respect to the central role of relationships in the healthy composition of personality by drawing attention to the fundamental importance of "attachment" itself in the primordial human experience of growth. Emotionally meaningful as well as intimate relationships constitute the bipartite core of human well-being and Bowlby described the centrality of attachment as essentially a biological system with an evolutionary history essential in the survival of the species. Evidence of just how crucial this biologically determined matrix of survival behavior is can be seen in instances where a child threatened with danger, estrangement, or emotional anxiety has a strong inclination to seek out members of the community amenable to providing intimate security and actual physical connectivity.

The general consensus among attachment theorists suggests four attachment styles or patterns to include security, anxiety-avoidance, anxiety-resistance, and disorganization with the first type of secure attachment suggesting a positive and trusting relationship with a selected caregiver. The anxiety-avoidance style of relationship is characterized by a deep and abiding sense of insecurity between child and caregiver implying a detectable sense of indifference towards the adult by the child. A third style of attachment identified by practitioners in the field is that of anxiety-resistance suggesting an elevated insecurity feeling between child and parent producing acute distress at the time of separation followed by feelings of anger at the point of reuniting whereas the fourth style of attachment labeled disorganization characterized devoid of patterned consistency in the parent/child relationship producing inevitably anxiety, stress, and tension in the interaction.

The natural inclination of human infants and children to seek out intimate attachments with others can be impeded when the child has been reared in the absence of such a nurturing *milieu* whether caused by *laissez faire* indifference or acute abuse and neglect. Predictably, the effects upon the infant and young child of the absence of such a nurturing experience often manifest themselves in dynamic expressions of undifferentiated anger, despair, feelings of detachment and stifled intellectual and cognitive development with the extended consequences into adulthood of accelerating unspecific aggression, a hovering and clinging pattern of failed attachment, or contrariwise acute detachment and emotional disorders with ever impending dynamic depression.

Within all of the various schools of research and theory in the field of developmental psychology has been the continuing undercurrent of issues and controversies regarding the relationship between genetic *speciel* (adjective form of the word *species*) characteristics and propensities versus the role and significance of the psycho-social, cultural, and physical environment of the developing child traditionally and popularly shortened to the "nature versus nurture" debate. Nativism versus empiricism is another shorthand term for this massively involved and researched debate and discussion. Whether genetically determined or environmentally conditioned, the debate has raged on but thanks to an increase in the research agenda on both sides the movement towards the center has commenced in full sway with a focus upon the complementarity of the issues rather than their competitive alternatives. Much of the rapprochement has been facilitated and advanced by the evolutionary perspective within development psychology.

Nowhere has this convergence of nature and nurture issues been more evidenced and research facilitated than in linguistics and the development of language. Language acquisition propensities may very well be a genetically wired characteristic of the human animal, but also there is strong evidence that the gaining of language proficiency is reflected in the human person's ability to acquire and assimilate language. If the nurture developmentalists of the empiricist school are correct, the procurement of linguistic capability and proficiency is provided by a learning environment through a process of developmental statistical learning such that commonly practiced learning methods are effective in teaching language. The proponents of the primacy of nature and genetics in the acquisition of language proficiency contend with a great deal of laboratory research standing with them that the complexities of a language structure are beyond the capability of an infant and early child to navigate and, therefore, with the famous linguist Noam Chomsky leading the discussion, there is clinical evidence of a universal grammar applicable and present in all human languages which is pre-specified. The nurture school having failed to provide equally convincing laboratory evidence of the central efficacy of the language input argument, growing inclination within contemporary developmental psychology is to pursue the concept of a special cognitive module relevant to the learning of language, i.e., called the "language acquisition device." Chomsky and company have been sufficiently persuasive with validating empirical data to precipitate a paradigm shift from the centrality of the behaviorist theory in spite of the lingering Skinnerian concept once very popular called "Verbal Behavior."

Though there is general agreement among psychologists working in the field of development that change is inevitable and it falls the responsibility of behavioral scientists to understand the mechanisms whereby such change occurs, there are a variety of differing perspectives with respect to the understanding of the nature of that inevitable change, its frequency, its intensity, and its duration with some theorists promoting a vision of developmental change as smooth and progressive which others contend for the sporadic, erratic, and irregular development over time. Whether one opts for the progressive perspective or the erratic perspective, there is general agreement that change does come and the study of that change, its character, its etiology, and its trajectory constitutes the agenda for developmental psychology as a specialization. An underlying theoretical concern is to what extent this inevitable change constitutes an ontological transformation of the individual himself/herself and, on the other hand, to what extent there is continuity within the human psyche from one stage of development to another such that the older adult is in some way the same person as the child from which the adult has emerged. Continuity versus transformation, then, is considered largely in the development theory agenda of lifespan psychologists.

Clearly change is inevitable and relentless and, therefore, presents a challenge to behavioral scientists in not only recognizing the occurrence of change but to more precisely understand the principles operative within the phenomenon of change itself and the construction of various interpretative schemes or constructs designed to configure an understanding of the dynamics of change occupies a great deal of research energy in developmental psychology. These schemes (or models) must function as an interpretive device to explain the nature and process of the inevitable changes which occur over time through the identified stages of development, whether one uses Freud or Erikson or Sullivan or any other recognized system based on descriptive stages of development. There are a variety of interpretive and research models used by developmental psychologists in the study of changes which occur over time within the individual including of particular popularity the mathematical model and what is commonly called the dynamic systems model (DSM).

The attractive feature of the mathematical model is its precision and ease of use covering the generation, explanation, integration, and prediction affecting the data gathered and analyzed in the developmental stages of the lifespan. The usefulness of the dynamic systems approach to modeling is that it has the capacity to integrate a plethora of complex data matrices producing a behavioral grid reflecting development. Something called "nonlinear dynamics," for instance, has been effective in the study of systemic progression in developmental stages of the lifespan including identifiable occurrences within the individual's transitional movements over time. This approach is proving particularly useful in analyzing the subtleties of such behavioral matrices as affect, life transitions, the acquisition of another language, and even mobility over the spectrum of the lifespan of development.

A major focus of research within developmental psychology is that of the cognitive dynamics operative within the infant and growing child particularly as relates to the acquisition and developmental usage of intrinsic mental capabilities including such features as problem-solving, memory, and the development of language. That which characterizes cognitive development studies primarily has to do with the learning of language and mobility skills and issues related to perception and manipulation and, of course, in this particular area as we shall see in Chapter Three of this book Jean Piaget is considered the dominant theorist. It was Piaget early on in the emergence of developmental psychology who emphasized with clinical evidence demonstrating the relevance of the developmental approach to the stages of the lifespan.

On the other hand, Lev Vygotsky and others have argued to the contrary that life does not proceed in identifiable developmental stages but rather the complexity of human growth and adaptation to the demands of life at various ages is too monumental in its variegation to submit to a progressively measured developmental stage scenario. Rather than a reliance upon the predictability of stage development, the post-Piaget developmentalists are demonstrating that cognitive growth and continued refinement of thought processes illustrate that such transitional events within the cognitive developmental process are linked to the efficient processing of information including the expansion of a working memory through lifespan development. Such factors allow for a more viable and robust differentiation in the study of childhood indicative of the variance of capabilities of children and, therefore, this trajectory of post-Piagetian research has led these developmental psychologists to move beyond the mechanistic concept of "stages of development" towards a more fluid appreciation and evaluation with a more lively recognition of the innateness of development over time.

Social psychologists have entered the discussion regarding development and this has broadened and strengthened the general field with particular relevance to the social development implied in lifespan researches. The factors of social and emotional skills development reflective of competent interaction influence such typical behavioral matrices as friendship development, emotion monitoring and assessment, and the emergence of a sense of self as self-identify in which cognitive development and social skills development converge and reflect a maturation process which is incremental yet sporadic and irregular in its progression. This sphere of research has produced a school of research called "emotional regulation" which focuses attention upon the monitoring and assessing of regulated emotional episodes confronted by the individual from infancy and childhood into adulthood and old age, moving from the inevitable external controls of behavior of the child by authority figures through the process of gradual accrual of responsibility for ones' self. ER seems to be directly related to the experience of the child related to parental and adult behaviors which are acceptable and non-acceptable within a social behavioral matrix of maturational progression into adulthood.

Within the context of emotional regulation, childhood social and emotional development are profoundly affected by what is called the "environmental stress hypothesis" (ESH) which suggests that how children manage their responses to emotional stress affects and is affected by their motor skills development such that developmental coordination difficulties are linked inextricably to their psychosocial environment. This matrix of stress inducing environmental encounters constitutes a fundamental etiology of depression and anxiety within children such that problems dealing with physical coordination issues become increasingly a debilitating factor in maturation of the child to adulthood. Practical manifestations of this emotionally deprived environment include evidence of a disinclination to participate as a child in physical play and particularly organized sports and the appearance of social loneliness due to under development of physical skills capabilities. Developmental psychologists emphasize six general areas of concern in this respect, viz., self-awareness, self-management, social awareness, relationship skills, responsible decision making, and a general sense of their own intellectual capabilities.

Both physical development and memory development have constituted the focus of much research attention owing to the central importance of the body's development over time from infancy to old age and the mental and physical changes which characterize this process. The physical maturation of an individual is more predictable under normal circumstances than is the individual's cognitive and emotional development. To disregard the fundamental importance of the physical changes the individual undergoes through the lifespan would be irresponsible. The incremental developmental characteristics of the maturation process is directly related to the mental and emotional development of the individual but just how they are linked constitutes a focus of much research, such factors as weight and height as well as strength and dexterity vary with every individual at every age but the linkage between the physical and the emotional/mental level of development is a crucial component of the overall understanding of progression through time. And not unrelated to this linkage between the body and the mind, the physical and the emotional development of the individual, is that of the nature and function as well as the development of the capacity for memory, and the distinctions and their importance between what is called verbatim or visual memory and gist memory or memory dependent solely upon words. The study of the transition in capability from visual to verbal memory over time constitutes a major field of investigation as this transition relates to the mental maturation over time from infancy to old age.

Thanks to the tremendous contribution Piaget has made to the advancement of developmental psychology in the study of children, research has constituted a fundamental occupation of behavioral scientists interested in the learning matrix of children. These researchers have focused upon experimental and correlational studies as well as the use of case studies. Since modern behavioral science is necessarily collaborative given the breadth as well as depth of the research communities involved in advancing our understanding of childhood learning, the sharing of information across a spectrum of research methods is to be expected. For instance, the experimental design model of research looks to the cause-and-effect relationship in the learning process such that the shuffling of variables as both independent and dependent constitutes a fundamental method of measurement granted the inevitable problematics of using controlled environments for study. To avoid the risk of contamination of the data caused by the difficulties of a controlled research environment, the correlational design method employs variable interactive relationships without the danger of interventionist contamination from researchers by virtue of its use of the natural learning environment though the limitation of this correlational approach is that it does not allow for the establishment of cause-and-effect relationships among the variables being studied. On the other hand, it is the case study approach which is designed to permit the research to gain an in-depth understanding of the research subject, the child in learning studies, based on the information gleaned with in-depth interviews and questionnaires along with acute observation. These three very popular design research methods, i.e., experimental, correlational, and case study, when working in tandem as a tripartite research system are very effective in identifying that for which each has addressed itself. The collaborative nature of this tripartite research design is characteristic of development psychologists' desire to be as comprehensive as possible in the study of child development.

While each of these research approaches are regularly configured as identifiable design techniques, i.e., logically constructed systemic configurations intended to create comparisons of data gathered in the tripartite process, there are four commonly recognized design constructs employed by developmental psychologists in their research schemes. They are classified as (1) longitudinal, (2) cross-sectional, (3) sequential, and (4) micro-genetic designs. In the first instance, longitudinal studies are designed for an extended period of study over time involving the same group of individuals with an aim of generalized findings applicable across the age spectrum. Though an extremely helpful research approach, the difficulties involve the large number of subjects required as well as major funding needed and the inevitable decline in the group being studied owing to human factors of death, illness, re-location, and loss of interest.

On the other hand, the second popular design is the cross-sectional study in which researchers attempt to distinguish individual characteristics of the various subjects from one another at any given time. In that case, fewer subjects are required and they need not be from the same locale or social *milieu*. However, these advantages are off-set by the disadvantage that commonality of life experience can vary considerably such that generalizations from the data become problematic. Though we will explore the micro-genetic design method developed by Piaget in Chapter Three, we should point out that the sequential design approach actually attempts to conflate both the longitudinal and cross-sectional methods into a single process whereby the researcher is able to study individuals from differing birth orders simultaneously tracking them over time and charting the identified changes and shifts in the group's development. The benefit of this confluence in method allows the researcher to understand and plot more clearly the differences between changes attributed to historical circumstances from those characteristics which have been determined to be essentially universal.

The distinguishing characteristic of the specialization of developmental psychology is known as the life stages of psychological or emotional development, and this has been the focus of much of this field of study since Freud first proposed the idea of developmental stages in the life cycle. However, whereas Freud's psychoanalytic interest focused on stages of emotional development such as the oral, anal, phallic, latent, and mature stages, in more recent years and since the major work of Karen Horney, Melanie Klein, Anna

Freud, Jean Piaget, Erik Erikson and particularly the work in interpersonal theory of personality by Harry Stack Sullivan, the refinement of these various strata of development has been quite elaborate with some discussion and even controversy over their complex gradations.

Beginning with prenatal development as the first strata of psychological and emotional growth in its earliest manifestations, these initial strata of the human person include three distinct sub-stages, viz., germinal, embryonic, and fetal stage. As we are concerned in this book with the "learning spectrum" of childhood, we will move quickly beyond these earliest stages to the more significantly relevant to our inquiry, namely, that of the stage of infancy with its sub-sets of development. Infancy is generally characterized by developmental psychologists as covering the first 12 months of the child's life and though there is some discussion and debate as to the details of this complex period of development, there is general consensus regarding the eventuation of diurnal sleep patterns after about the first two or three months. Subsequently, there is a recognized set of sleep-and-awake behavioral patterns consisting of six states paired into three sets, namely, (1) quiet and active sleep patterns including dreaming; (2) quiet and active waking states; and (3) fussing and crying behavior, all of which any parent would be most familiar.

During these crucial few months of initial development, infant perception, language accrual, and cognition constitute the three key aspects of the maturation process which developmental psychologists have chosen to focus their attention upon and each of which are more or less detectable by the attentive parent or child care provider. The early infant's perception consists of the human components of the five senses, that is, what he/she can see, hear, smell, taste, and touch, and each sense develops at its own speed with sometimes considerable variances between them. These variances constitute a major focus and concern of the health care provider for it is during these early months when problems and issues related to stifled development can be detected, such as a failure of visual acuity or cognitive responsiveness. Whereas danger signs with respect to vision and hearing are readily detectable by the attending physician as well as attentive parent, with adult-level vision capability on the part of the healthy infant being reached within six months of birth and hearing at the adult-level within 18 months, olfactory and tactile senses develop more specifically with reference to the mother. Studies show that the infant early on prefers the proximity of its mother owing to her unique aroma and handling of the infant, subtle but significant indicators of development.

Within this development matrix of the one-year-old infant, and due to a healthy auditory sense, the infant quickly develops a linguistic acuity allowing for both variation in their own noise-making as well as detection in the voice sounds of those around it, particularly the mother and care givers versus strangers (and even different languages which some studies have shown to be particularly telling when an infant is cared for intermittently by individuals speaking different languages). Though we will explore in greater detail the work of Jean Piaget and his research team in the sophisticated development of a cognitive theory of child maturation which has dominated the field of developmental psychology for nearly a half century, we should at this juncture point out that Piaget's understanding of the early infant's perception capacity is dependent upon the child's motor development. What he called the sensorimotor stage of development, Piaget demonstrated clinically in his laboratory that the linkage of vision and touch was essentially in object identification and the resulting learning curve of object endurance over time even when not present to the infant at any given time such that as the infant matures there is the realization that when one's mother is absent she will return. Reassurance of this fact to the infant Harry Stack Sullivan has suggested is crucial in avoiding the development of a neurotic anxiety which might very well be carried into adulthood.

Though developmental psychology has advanced our understanding of this cognitive development in the early days of the infant's life such that much of what Piaget has done is now being modified, corrected, and enhanced, there is the inevitability in the rearing of children for there to be what is now called "developmental delays" owing both to physical factors in the child as well as and most importantly in the psycho-social environment of the maturation period of growth. Thanks to Sullivan and subsequent work precipitated by the early developmentalists such as Horney, Klein, and Erikson all building on the work of Anna Freud, we understand more fully the role of the physical learning environment of the child as relates to a healthy or unhealthy maturation. We now know much more about the centrality of proper social environmental learning matrices such that the child manifesting developmental delay (DD) in some aspect of maturation will more likely develop behavioral and emotional complications in interpersonal relationships than the child who does not experience such developmental delays, sometimes labeled typical development (TD). The psychopathology of developmental delays now constitutes one of the major research fields of study within developmental psychology which has called into play more than ever the interfacing of psychological and physiological data for analysis and diagnosis of mental disorders identified early in a child's life.

There is a nuanced period between childhood *per se* and infancy recognized and researched by developmental psychologists labeled "toddlerhood" most conspicuously characterized by the emergence of a sense of self, a self-awareness in which maturation is bringing on linguistic capabilities facilitated by an increased capacity for memory and imagination. Mobility of movement and decision-making choices affecting their expressive preferences characterizes these few months of development and most outstandingly observable is the interest in and experimentation with audiation (singsong speech) and the use of intentional language understood to be the primary mechanism for communication with "others," the interpersonal skills development is linked to the development and refinement of language precision. Not only in speech is the child exploratory and experimental but the drive towards adventure not infrequently resulting in errors or mistakes or even mishaps all converging upon the cognitive capacities of the toddler in the learning process of maturation.

Much of the value and benefit of this strong adventurous propensity can either be elevated by the caring and nurturing parent or caregiver interested in facilitating the toddler's courageous outreach into the environment or it can be stifled and truncated by the overprotective or disapproving parent or caregiver more interested either in the child's safety from harm or impeding the inevitable demands made by the growing child. The former style of parenting enhances the child's self-awareness of the environment and self-confidence of his place in it whereas the latter becomes a monumental deterrent to the child's normal growth and development, the stifling of which may have long-lasting negative affects upon the young adult. Guilt, fear, shame and self-worthlessness become the natural reaction to such stifling of the natural inclinations of the toddler to explore, and this negative experience quite decidedly affects the perception of the toddler's gender identity. Frustration resulting from a failure of the parent or caregiver to understand the desires and intentions of the toddler, especially when the child is attempting to communicate however ineffectively through speech, is a common characteristic of this time period and has unfortunately been labeled the "terrible twos" to reflect the unsettling nature of this stage of maturation.

The first four stages of development of Erik Erikson's eight stage schema deals with childhood from infancy through to the school age of 12 years old. Not using the now common term of toddler, Erikson listed the four stages of childhood to be that of infancy to 1 ½ years in which the choice is trust versus mistrust, early childhood from 2 ½ to 3 wherein the psychosocial crisis of maturation (every stage Erikson believed was precipitated by a maturational crisis) was that between autonomy and shame and doubt, the play stage being from 3 to 5 years of age (called by most psychologists as pre-school age) wherein the crisis is between initiative and guilt and the fourth and final stage of childhood Erikson labeled school age from 5 to 12 years of age in which the crisis of development is between industry and inferiority. By lumping infancy and the toddler stages together, we move to the play stage or preschool years of 3 to 5 during which time the social skills they learned from their parents and siblings now confront a challenge in facing an increase in size and number of persons with whom interaction is necessary.

The result of this expansive world is the furtherance of operational thinking facilitated to the extent that the development is a deepening capacity for a positive relationship and *repertoire*. Independence at this stage is aided by virtue of increased physical dexterity and mobility and, thus, the preschooler is able to confront a wider scope of people and expectations during which time the learning curve about the world and the things and people in it takes an exponential jump forward. During this time period, play itself becomes crucial for cognitive development and is directly linked to these growing experiences of diversity and challenge, excitement and exploration. Erikson is insistent upon the crucial nature of the parental nurturing of the pre-school child as relates to encouraging exploration and adventure wherein personal initiative comes into play for the healthy child or, alas, the emergence of a debilitating sense of guilt for the stifled child who fails the psychosocial crisis of the 3-5 year old according to Erikson's model.

The movement from infancy to toddlerhood is incrementally small with respect to the maturation process leading to interactive communication skills and physical dexterity, but the leap from toddlerhood and preschool age children to the commencement of what is recognized as childhood and the school years is monumentally dynamic in the acceleration of psycho-social skills development and cognitive processes. Covering ages 6 to 12, the middle childhood years have been characterized by Erikson as the differentiation between creative initiative or the converse as a sense of diminished worth within the social matrix of school age self-identity. One has a developed awareness of personal competency in facing society and the world or one has failed, owing to a variety of psycho-social factors, to develop a sense of personal value and worth.

The inculcation of a self of personal worthiness and intrinsic value occurs within the school environment fostered by peers and teachers alike. Even the process of learning and examinations as well as corporate activities such as sports and games constitutes the matrix for growth or, where these things are dysfunctional and inoperative within the life of a child, the matrix for failure, a diminishment of self-worth or a failure to develop a sense of self-worth which can and usually does follow the child into adulthood with the impending personality disorders which accompany this failure during the school years. Unwittingly, the overly critical parent or teacher can undermine the child's normal development by fostering a sense of inadequacy and inferiority such that the child, instead of having these years be the cultivation of a solid sense of self-worth and overt capabilities to face society and the world is rather saddled with a weakened self-awareness and feelings of impending failure. The psycho-social environment constitutes the matrix within which success or failure is initially established and nurtured in the school-age child.

In order to more clearly define the complexities of these years, the Centers for Disease Control have actually divided these years into two sub-sets labeled the Middle Childhood stage one (6-8) and the Middle Childhood stage two (9-11), the overlapping being intentional owing to the differences in developmental processes among children, particularly between boys and girls. Stage one sees the child investigating his/her place in the world and anticipating what the future may hold as the child navigates through the social maze of friendship and independence from parents and siblings. These stage one days of middle childhood see the acceleration of linguistic *finesse* as well as exploratory usage of language which did not exist or quite commonly was forbidden in the family environment and the subtle but crucial movement away from unrestrained narcissism towards a more robust sense of camaraderie and sharing of ideas and activities with one's peers. The second stage of middle childhood goes further in the cultivation of solid friendships and interpersonal relationships of an increasing complexity and inevitably a susceptibility to the expectations of one's newly acquired associates in the form of peer pressure, a new experience and one which must be negotiated with care. The skills required for learning continue to develop and accrue such that the balancing of different and even competing and conflicting ideas about right and wrong, true and false, fairness and deceit, all becomes factors needing attention, selection, and integration in the maturing middle childhood years.

The turbulent years of adolescence from the bucolic days of pre-adolescence to the ending of school days of the late adolescence/early adulthood are characterized by many factors but none so central as that of the on-set of puberty. Though covering about an 8 or 9 year span from what is labeled Early Adolescence (9 to 13) through Middle Adolescence (13 to 15) concluding in Late Adolescence (15 to 18), this tripartite stratification of the maturation process of the post-childhood individual constitutes one of the most research fields in developmental psychology owing to the complexities of each of the sub-set age groups. The turmoil usually experienced by the individual reaching puberty is fraught with stress, anxiety, uncertainty, and outright confusion as to what is happening to them and why. It is during these crucial years of physical maturity that the individual becomes increasingly aware of and responsive to a sense of personal identity (or lack thereof) and a genuine responsiveness to issues related to moral behavior, the right and wrong of decisions needing to be made within the framework of social responsibility. What it means to be a man or a woman and how that is lived out through the process of social interaction with others constitutes an abiding fixation in the emotional life of the adolescent. Within this context, intellectual acuity has an opportunity to expand to cover the growing range of issues related to information needed for meaningful decision-making activity.

Discovering what is meant by reasonable and how to employ reason in decision-making situations constitutes a significant growth arena for the maturing adolescent. This is the time more profoundly affecting the trajectory of the individual into adulthood than during childhood. Questions about identity and destiny and the ever impending dangers of loss of a sense of self and role confusion constitute the growth environment of the adolescent approaching adulthood.

Having more or less successfully navigated through the turbulent years of early/mid/late adolescence, the individual confronts the inevitability of adulthood with all of its impending demands and expectations, challenges and opportunities for growth and happiness. The early days of adulthood treated by developmental psychologists are commonly considered to cover ages 18 to 29 and normally focused fundamentally upon the establishment and maintenance of meaningful relationships stratified at various levels of intimacy and camaraderie. The culturally validated end-goal is usually that of creating a family but the urgency and relevance of that goal is very much dictated by the young adult's social network as well as family tradition. During these early days of adulthood, the formation of personality and relationship skills developed during adolescence become crucial for it is in this stage of life when the quality of maturation manifests itself most profoundly and where there was a failure or breakdown in adolescent maturation mental illness is more commonly to appear at this stage of life. Harry Stack Sullivan and the interpersonal theory of personality contends with much clinical evidence in support that the etiology of mental illness is directly linked to the failure of the development of interpersonal skills in childhood owing to parental indifference, ineptitude, or inadequacy in child care (Morgan, 2015, 2016, 2017, 2018, 2019). Where failure in relationship skills development is evidenced there is the presence of a sense of isolation, fear of commitment, and a diminished sense of self-worth such that a plethora of personality disorders are more likely to appear at this time.

Before moving to the middle adulthood years normally set in industrialized societies as between 29 and 49 years of age, we should pause to say a few things of relevance in developmental psychology about the parenting of children since it is customarily during these years that the family is established. For developmental psychologists, issues surrounding parenting are crucial owing to the clinical evidence that upwards of half of the variances reflected in child maturation are related to parenting itself. Though Sullivan has had much to say about this reality, clinical evidence is now replete with validation of the over-all characterization of the relevance and central importance of parents to the successful adjustment of children in adulthood. The etiology of adult mental illness is linked substantially to the parent-child relationship from infancy through childhood.

What is now labeled as parenting styles constitutes a major orientation of developmental psychology's focus upon child development and though there is a range of sub-sets within the parenting style matrix, four are generally recognized as universally normative in modern societies, i.e., authoritative parenting, authoritarian parenting, permissive parenting, and neglectful parenting. The first of these traditional styles of raising a child called authoritative parenting constitutes the best of the options for this approach to child-rearing and is characterized by a genuine sense of interactive involvement between parent and child with heavy emphasis upon warmth and responsiveness with a minimum of discipline and negative supervision. Studies show that the end result of this approach is that the child gains strength in self-confidence and openness to the opportunities presented to them through social interaction and exploration of their living environment. On the other hand, authoritarian parenting style creates an environment of fear, anxiety, distrust, and suspicion in the absence of encouragement and parental warmth such that the child is much more tentative in facing the world of social expectations and much more likely to develop dysfunctional relationships in adulthood. While raised in a casual and non-directive environment, the child in the permissive parenting environment will find that owing to the absence of guidance and expectations of increasing signs of maturity, there will be a stifling of progression towards responsible adulthood with a delay in cognitive development as well. The child raised in the neglectful parenting environment, while experiencing a diminished level of expectations and responsibilities, finds himself disconnected to the emotional and intimate life of the parents without firm structures for maturing with the result that these children are the least developed of all four categories of parenting styles.

It is during these middle adulthood of 29 to 49 years that the individual begins to struggle with the competing forces of creativity and stagnation in which the feelings of failure to have contributed to the well-fare of the family and society or pride in accomplishment constitute the defining scope of this developmental period. Owing to the demands of these middle years including work expectations and family commitments, the individual gradually begins to experience a decline in physical vitality even when, as is common among the middle class, individuals begin to exert themselves in efforts to stave off the aging process through gymnastics and cosmetics. Women begin to ponder and anticipate menopause with a national average of 48.8 years of age and the inevitable decline in hormone estrogen production while men commonly experience a decline in the endocrine system and libido diminishment. These middle adulthood years see the highest levels of depression until the on-set of old age.

Controversy around the world within the medical and psychological communities has to do with when "old age" actually commences with the World Health Organization preferring to avoid the formal designation of the age range but is+ inclined to suggest that within developing societies individuals are commonly designated having entered the category of older people between 60 and 65 years. The general descriptive characteristics include the recognition that the individual has ceased or is diminishing in the ability to make an identified and measurable contribution to society at large and the family specifically rather than just relying upon chronological age. Individuals self-identifying with this designation in their lifespan have a tendency to be increasingly reflective about their life, their successes and their failures, pondering the unrealized dreams of adventure and valuing those episodes of real joy and happiness such as they are. Depending on how the scale balances with respect to this reflection, there may be the on-set of debilitating depression especially when accompanied by a measurable decline in physical capabilities including muscular dexterity and aptitude as well as such factors as hearing loss and visual diminishment, even the sense of taste and smell may be recognized as in decline with, of course, the inevitable life-threatening illnesses such as cancer, stroke, heart failure, and increasingly important the on-set of dementia and Alzheimer's disease with men beginning at about age 79 and women at 82. It is generally agreed within the profession of developmental psychology that much more needs to be done in terms of developing of a theoretical construct designed specifically to address the post-retirement population owing to its increasing size and influence in American society and industrial societies generally. Most psychological models are very effective from infancy to retirement as they have been more or less developed when life expectancy anticipated demise soon after retirement. However, today we see a large portion of the population living 20 to 30 years beyond retirement and the psychological as well as medical communities are struggling to understand how best to respond to emotional issues which now arise during these last two or three decades of the retirement population's life.

Chapter Two

Marie Montessori (1870-1952) And Scientific Pedagogy

The irony regarding Marie Montessori is that on the one hand she is recognized as one of the most important educators in the 20th century while on the other hand very little attention or acknowledgment of her actual contribution to developmental psychology as relates to children has been recognized by the wider scientific community. No name has as extensive a recognition in the field of education as has Montessori and yet when examining the textbooks dealing with the psychological development of children, she is seldom mentioned. In many respects, Montessori is to pedagogy what Freud is to psychology. Granted, there are many retractors and not a few who have adopted and then adapted both systems of theory and research to their own ends and the scientific communities in both education and psychology have unquestionably been the beneficiaries. With that being said, not much if any of the advancements in pedagogy and psychotherapy could have happened without Montessori and Freud first appearing on the scene. That both were trained physicians who chose to move outside the comfort zone of their respective professions is an indication of both their courage and creativity, Montessori into education and Freud into psychoanalysis. In the following, we will examine closely the tremendous contributions to the theory of scientific pedagogy Montessori has made and their relevance to the field of developmental psychology and particularly the learning spectrum in child development.

Born August 31, 1870 in the Italian town of Chiaravalle, Maria Tecla Artemisia Montessori, was the daughter of an official of the Italian Ministry of Finance, Alessandro Montessori, and Renilde Stoppani, the great-niece of the famous Italian geologist and paleontologist Antonio Stoppani. Though close to both of her parents emotionally, she very much resisted her father's discouragement of her desire to become a physician, something at the time quite unheard of for a girl to consider becoming for there was no educational track for such an ambition. She began her formal education in a public elementary school in Rome in 1876 and records show that though she received a certificate for good behavior she was not a particularly outstanding student but managed to complete her formal public education with good grades in 1886 at the age of 16. Continuing her education beyond the required years, she studied a full range of subjects from art to zoology as well as French and German but distinguished herself in the sciences and mathematics. At age 20 she completed her studies at the polytechnic and had changed her professional aspirations from that of becoming an engineer (having been influenced unduly by parental pressure) to that of medicine, a field unknown to women at the time.

While receiving strong discouragement from the medical faculty at the University of Rome to whom she had made an appeal for admittance, she did become a student at the University taking courses in natural sciences with successful examinations passed in botany, zoology, experimental physics, anatomy, and chemistry during which time she earned the *Diploma de Licenza* in 1892, a credential that qualified her for entry into the medical school in 1893. She developed the habit of smoking so as to cover the terrible odors of the dissection laboratory which she was forced to inhabit after hours owing to the resistance of students and faculty over having her present in the laboratory with men students and the naked cadavers being used. In spite of all and owing to her tenacity, she won an academic award her first year and the following year was granted a post as a hospital assistant, a position she needed for her clinical experience. The remaining two years were spent in pediatrics and psychiatry in which she distinguished herself in pediatric medicine, graduating from the University of Rome School of Medicine in 1896. With the publication of her doctoral thesis in the distinguished Italian journal *Policlinico,* she was employed by the University hospital in Rome as a medical assistant at which time she also established a private practice in general medicine and pediatrics. During the next five years she became an outspoken advocate for women's rights and access to medical education as well as an international spokesperson for the development of educational programs designed specifically for children suffering from mental disabilities and mental illness combining these activities with her appointment as a medical researcher at the University's psychiatric clinic working with children.

Owing to the restrictions socially placed upon women at the time such that if they were married they were not permitted to work professionally but rather were expected to stay at home, Montessori chose not to marry the man she loved, Giuseppe Montesano, M.D., with whom she had a son in 1898, Mario Montessori. Her partner was at the time a co-director with her of the Orthophrenic School of Rome, a center for the study and treatment of mentally ill and disabled children. The secrecy of their relationship was maintained until Dr. Montesano fell in love with someone else leaving Montessori bereft necessarily precipitating her decision to leave medical practice at the University hospital and placing her child in foster care during his childhood and adolescent years. Eventually reuniting with him during his teens, he became a key research assistant to her and her work. At this point, her reputation was gaining her national and even international attention as an advocate for children suffering from mental disease and disabilities such that in 1897 she was invited to give an address on societal responsibilities for juvenile delinquents at the National Congress of Medicine in Turin.

The following year and after publishing several scholarly articles on the subject, she was invited to make a presentation before the First Pedagogical Conference of Turin in which she called for both the establishment of public institutions for the care of mentally disabled children as well as the development of a training curriculum for the caregivers at these institutions. Initially appointed a counselor and subsequently a member of the board of the newly created National League for the Protection of Retarded Children which she herself assisted in creating, she was in 1899 appointed to the faculty of two teacher-training colleges for women in Italy in the fields of hygiene and anthropology. By this time and before she turned 30 years of age, she was an internationally recognized authority in this field of research and study and was in demand throughout Europe and the United States as a speaker on the subject of child care and education.

Partially in answer to her calls for such an initiative, in 1900 the National League created a medical and pedagogical institution for the training of teachers in the care of mentally disabled children called the *Scuola Magistale Ortofrenica* which also included a first-of-its-kind laboratory classroom with Montessori appointed co-director of this facility. With an initial enrollment of school teachers of over 60 taking courses in psychology, anatomy, physiology, and anthropology related to pediatric mental disabilities, Montessori in this environment was assisted in the development of new methods of instruction and materials initially designed for children with mental disabilities but subsequently modified for a full spectrum of children. So successful was this experiment that both the Italian government and the University of Rome began to pay close attention to these innovative ideas of education using Montessori's model classroom as a paradigm for implementation in the Italian public schools for all children.

Surprising everyone but indicative of her original thinking, Montessori resigned from the Orthophrenic School and gave up her private medical practice to enter the University of Rome in 1892 to pursue a degree in philosophy (which at the time included psychology as a major component of the curriculum). As she began to envision adapting her insights and philosophy to a broader spectrum of educational opportunities in working with mentally healthy children as well as the disabled, she commenced referencing her perspective as "scientific pedagogy" in a series of papers published over a short period of time resulting in her being appointed a faculty lecturer in the Pedagogic School at the University of Rome where she continued teaching until 1908. During these productive years she published her essays in book form titled *Pedagogical Anthropology* (1910) and also took on the responsibility of developing what eventually she would formalize as a children's house of education for working-class and low-income parents in a poor neighborhood in Rome called officially *Casa dei Bambini.* The historic importance of this initiative cannot be over-stated for it is within the matrix of this laboratory environment that the Montessori system of *scientific pedagogy* found its first expression and with major success from the very beginning of its implementation.

Judging from today's perspective and what we know and have learned about child development, what Montessori did in her first laboratory classroom would be considered quite simplistic and elementary. However, at the time the Children's House educational program (called officially the *Orthophrenic School*) was extremely adventurous and experimental owing to the lack of any pedagogical research available at that time. The setting, props, and equipment was quite simple and pragmatic. There was a teacher's table and blackboard, a stove for heating the classroom, little chairs for the small children, some armchairs for teachers, staff, and observing parents, a compilation of small tables grouped together for the children's use, a materials cabinet under lock and key, and beyond that nothing else.

Besides the basic classroom furnishings and environment, Montessori was keen to implement a program of orchestrated activities for the children of value to their own personal care and development such as learning how to dress themselves, taking care of their living and learning environment such as sweeping and even so far as learning how to care for flowers in the garden, i.e., activities with a practical purpose. Though she did not engage in the teaching itself, she was particularly involved in the development herself of educational materials which otherwise were not available and these were specifically based on her own research and observations related to goals and aspirations created through staff/pupil collaborations. The coupling of a specifically designed learning environment with particularly developed learning activities constituted the matrix out of which Montessori's philosophy of education found expression and resulted in the creation of what would eventually become the Montessori scientific pedagogical method.

Montessori's gift of observation served her well owing to her training both in pediatrics and in psychology which enabled her to note and value the young child's ability and inclination to maintain acute attention and concentration on a topic combined with the effective use of repetitive activities characterized by a natural tendency to order and system in the young child learner. These features she identified and elevated to a strata of relevant insights into the natural learning propensities of little children which to-date had not been recognized by traditional teaching methods in the public schools of Italy. Innovative and pioneering observations characterized Montessori's approach to the continued development of this scientific pedagogy such that she was able to demonstrate the child's natural proclivity to the engagement of practical and pragmatic activities when given a choice and a preference, quite enlightening to the traditionalist, for the materials created and developed by her rather than the manufactured toys commonly provided to little children. A shocking discovery based on fundamental observation of children's behavior was their disinclination to be motivated by the offering of candy as a rewarding mechanism. The gradual but easily identified inclination towards self-discipline within the behavioral arena of the child's expressive purview proved most insightful as to motivation and constructive as to the future design of space and curriculum in the school.

Coming out of this first innovative experimental approach to the education of the young child were a variety of what would become standard operational policies and procedures in the development of future learning environments reflective of the emerging Montessori method and pedagogical philosophy. For instance, what now seems simple and pragmatic was the decision to replace heavy furnishings with light weight chairs and tables so the children could exercise some jurisdiction over space control and the replacing of regular height table with low and easily accessible tables and shelves making the classroom "child responsive" rather than convenient for the teacher. She expanded the practical and pragmatic range of activities designed for both exercise and the fulfillment of a valued function such as caring for the flower garden at the school, washing one's hands regularly as a practical concern for hygiene and going so far as to engage in modest but meaningful cooking activities. Montessori paid close attention to the actual utilization of space in the learning environment so rather than having rows of desks and chairs she created an openness in the classroom with work stations along the walls highlighting the spaciousness of the room's center allowing for ease of movement by the child from one station to another as the child was so inclined. The day began for the child at 9 a.m. and ended at 4 p.m. and she organized the day in one hour increments as illustrated here:

- 9–10. Entrance. Greeting. Inspection as to personal cleanliness. Exercises of practical life; helping one another to take off and put on the aprons. Going over the room to see that everything is dusted and in order. Language: Conversation period: Children give an account of the events of the day before. Religious exercises.
- 10–11. Intellectual exercises. Objective lessons interrupted by short rest periods. Nomenclature, Sense exercises.
- 11–11:30. Simple gymnastics: Ordinary movements done gracefully, normal position of the body, walking, marching in line, salutations, movements for attention, placing of objects gracefully.
- 11:30–12. Luncheon: Short prayer.
- 12–1. Free games.
- 1–2. Directed games, if possible, in the open air. During this period the older children in turn go through with the exercises of practical life, cleaning the room, dusting, putting the material in order. General inspection for cleanliness: Conversation.
- 2–3. Manual work. Clay modelling, design, etc.
- 3–4. Collective gymnastics and songs, if possible in the open air. Exercises to develop forethought: Visiting, and caring for the plants and animals.

The overall philosophical postulate centered around the concept of the child "working independently" such that through the freely and generously supported sense of independence and autonomy of movement and the pursuit of personally selected activities based on the belief that children are naturally motivated to continually expand their knowledge and understanding of the environment and the world around them. This was, for the time, a radical notion of empowering the child to explore their own capacities for learning rather than the instructional model of teacher-tell/student-listen approach. This method characterized virtually all of the modern world's approach to early childhood education such that "independence" itself became a stated goal of education with the teacher being an observer and facilitator of the child's own learning initiative and interests.

Needless to say, the first school was an unequivocal success and, therefore, there was a second such school as the *Casa dei Bambini* opened in 1907 with Montessori's continued furtherance of the philosophy of independent learning and self-discipline on the part of young children. The reported results of such a pedagogical approach begin to gain national attention among the education establishment in Italy itself including government officials and journalists. Furthering her quest to expand this scientific pedagogical model to include both reading and writing skills for the young child, she began to develop materials designed specifically to encourage and enhance language knowledge, experimenting with flash cards and paper cutouts with positive results of children learning to actually read much earlier than traditional techniques had done.

The following year three more Montessori schools opened and in 1909 the Swiss government began to substitute the Montessori school method to replace their traditional methods employed in state-run orphanages as well as kindergartens. The inevitable eventuality saw the offering of the first Montessori methods teaching course offered in Italy in 1909 concurrent with the publication of her first book explicating this new method of teaching titled *The Method of Scientific Pedagogy Applied to the Education of Children in the Children's Houses.* Following this success was the offering of such a training course in Rome in 1910 and in Milan in 1911 and the resulting termination of her private medical practice to give herself over entirely to the further development of her methods through research, writing, and particularly the offering of training courses for teachers. She eventually resigned her position on the faculty at the University of Rome as well in order to release her from duties other than the promotion of her method. Having begun to attract international attention, the Montessori Method, as it was being labeled, began to appear in Italy, Switzerland, the United Kingdom as well as France where in Paris Montessori Schools were being established. In London, Johannesburg, and Stockholm Montessori Schools were being established leading to the creation of Montessori Societies called in the United States the Montessori American Committee and in England the Montessori Society for the United Kingdom. The first International Training Course in the Montessori Method was held in Rome in 1913 followed in 1914 with another such conference.

Publishing her work was a major concern for Montessori and the United States. Her first book titled, *the Montessori Method,* was published and became a best seller with subsequent editions published in England and Switzerland the same year, 1913, when it appeared in Russia and Poland and enjoyed six subsequent editions with modifications and additions as Montessori continued to refine her methodology. In rapid annual succession, this book appeared in translation in Germany, Japan, Romania, Span, Holland, and Denmark. Furthermore, her second major book titled *Pedagogical Anthropology* was actually published in English as well as her practical guide to the didactic materials she had been developing titled *Montessori's Own Handbook*. Her popularity in the United States was especially enhanced by the publication of a series of articles in *McClure's Magazine* precipitating the opening of the North American Montessori School in Tarrytown, New York, the first of what would be thousands of American schools subsequently being established. Montessori became a real success in the United States owing partially to Mrs. Alexander Graham Bell's championing of this method in her Canadian home due to a visit by Montessori in 1913 on a lecture tour which she repeated in 1915, this time sponsored by the National Education Association.

In 1915, she made a major presentation at the Panama-Pacific International Exposition in San Francisco, California, and though her method was becoming increasingly recognized and applauded she was not without detractors and enduring controversy including a dismissive attack by a well-known American educator William Heard Kilpatrick, a disciple of John Dewey, who wrote a scathing critique titled *The Montessori Method Examined*. Regrettably, the National Kindergarten Association in the U.S. was likewise critical of what was thought to be Montessori's personality traits. She did insist upon a very strong control over any attempt to expand or elaborate on her system without her approval and certainly no one was allowed to offer Montessori teacher training except herself. No material not developed by Montessori herself personally was allowed to be referred to as Montessorian such that after her 1915 departure from the U.S. there was a distinct hiatus of interest in her method until her death in 1952 when her pedagogical system was reinvigorated by a new generation of educators and psychologists.

However, her returning to Europe in 1915 saw her method increasingly popular among European educators and after moving to Barcelona, Spain, where she made her new home. For the next 20 years she immersed herself in promoting her scientific pedagogy resulting in the massive expansion of her followers in the creation of new schools throughout Spain, the Netherlands, the United Kingdom, and Italy. The Spanish government actually developed an Escola Montessori which addressed the needs of three to ten year old children as well as creating a research, training, and teaching institution. A fourth international course she offered for teachers of six to twelve year olds focusing on grammar, math, and geometry which resulted in 1917 in the publication in Italian and English of her book *The Advanced Montessori Method*. Regrettably due to political turmoil within Spain of the Catalan independence movement, her work was terminated though she continued to make Barcelona her home for the next dozen years. Spain in 1933, now on solid political footing again, created a new training course in the Montessori Method which the government itself backed financially but, alas, the Civil War in Spain in 1936 put an end to these initiatives such that she left Spain never to return.

Successful initiatives in both the Netherlands and the United Kingdom colored Montessori's endeavors over the next twenty years in those countries beginning in 1917 with the creation of the Netherlands Montessori Society and her inaugural lecture in Amsterdam subsequently giving a series of such lectures at the University of Amsterdam in 1920. Within a decade there were over 200 Montessori schools in the country and the influence was so encouraging that the International Montessori Association (AMI) set its permanent offices in Amsterdam. During these blissful days of expansion of her educational philosophy, Montessori had to deal with the controversies created in the United States and exported to England such that her influence there was somewhat stifled and less than enthusiastically received as she had been through Europe, especially the Netherlands, Spain, and Italy, though she continued offering successfully training courses periodically in England into the commencement of World War II. Italy presented a more complicated story overall due to the ups and downs of the Italian government's volatility. Initially and under the influence of the Fascist government headed by Benito Mussolini himself the year following a 1922 course of lectures sponsored by the government, Montessori returned to Italy under government sponsorship when she received formal validation of her work by the ministry of education who had given official support of the Montessori Schools of Italy as well as her teacher training program.

In 1924, Mussolini himself following a formal one-on-one meeting with Montessori gave his official support of the Montessori Method as part of the national educational program such that there resulted in the creation of the Society of Friends of the Montessori Method as well as the Montessori Society with a government-issued Charter making Montessori herself the honorary president of the organization. While it lasted, this official support was splendid for the movement such that in 1927 there was the formal establishment of the Montessori Teacher Training College with government supported Montessori institutes throughout the country. But, alas, soon thereafter from 1930 onwards there was ideological turmoil with the Fascist government over Montessori's lectures on Peace and Education resulting in both herself and her son being placed under political surveillance. She formally left Italy in 1934 and the Italian government terminated all Montessori initiatives and programs throughout the country.

Montessori's now famous 1923 Vienna lecture was subsequently published in English in 1936 as *The Child in the Family*. During the past 20 years Montessori schools had been created in twenty-five countries around the world. Reflecting this international expansion was the 1929 hosting by Elsinore, Denmark, the First International Montessori Congress at which time Mario Montessori, her son, founded the International Montessori Association (AMI). As a governing body for all institutions and schools claiming to be Montessori in philosophy and practice, it maintained complete jurisdiction legally over all publications of Montessori's books and materials. Amazingly, three of the greatest sponsors of the AMI were Sigmund Freud, Jean Piaget, and Rabindranath Tagore. The International Peace Club of Geneva, Switzerland, published a lecture she had given in 1932 on peace and education at the Second International Montessori Congress in Nice, France, which was followed by a host of lectures on the relationship of peace to education throughout a troubling time in Europe resulting in her being nominated six times during her life for the Nobel Peace Prize.

It was 1936 when the Montessoris left Barcelona and eventually arrived in Laren near Amsterdam, after a short stay in England, where she would live the remainder of her life. During these last years in Amsterdam, she and her son Mario worked tirelessly on continued improvements, advancements, and expansions of her written materials and new editions of her books. Owing to the political turmoil now smothering Europe, Montessori focused increasingly upon issues related to peace and education and the interrelationship of the two. She went so far as to call for the development of what she called a "science of peace" which gained her increasing international recognition such that the Theosophical Society, for instance, invited her to India to offer a training program for teachers there on the subject. Her impact in India was profoundly nurtured by Tagore himself who was establishing Tagore-Montessori Schools all over India following the creation of the Montessori Society of India as early as 1926.

Owing to political turmoil between India and the United Kingdom with the Italians siding with the Germans, Montessori was detained in India until 1946 following the end of World War II. Never letting up on the continued development and broadening application of the Montessori philosophy of education, she and her son Mario under the cultural influence of their stay in India. They developed what came to be called "cosmic education" for children ages six to twelve with a focus on the international interconnectedness of all people with the natural environment which called for the teaching of botany, zoology, and geography. The result was the publication of two more books, *Education for a New World* and *To Educate the Human Potential*. Following the offering of some thirty lectures on her new study of infancy (to age three) sponsored by the Sri Lanka government resulting in her newest book titled *What You Should Know About Your Child,* she and her family left for Europe following attendance at the All India Montessori Conference in Jaipur.

Making her residential home permanently in Amsterdam at the age of 76 in 1946, she continued to lecture and travel throughout Europe and happily established a training institute in London in 1946 called the Montessori Centre. The following year she was back in India presenting the Four Plans of Development explicated in her new book *The Absorbent Mind* followed the next year with *The Discovery of the Child.* At the 8th International Montessori Congress in Italy in 1949, a training course was established for teachers of children from infancy to three years old called the Montessori School for Assistants to Infancy. Nominated for the Nobel Peace Prize that year, she was awarded the French Legion of Honor, Officer of the Dutch Order of Orange Nassau, and an honorary doctorate from the University of Amsterdam. In 1951 she made a presentation in London at the 9th International Montessori Congress and died of a brain hemorrhage in the Netherlands the following year on May 6, 1952.

THE MONTESORRI METHOD: Scientific Pedagogy

Regrettably, Marie Montessori in spite of her international fame as an innovative educator is not commonly listed among educational or developmental psychologists as a leading figure. There is some uncertainty as to why not owing to the creative genius recognized in her work by the international community of educators, all of whom are reliant upon developmental psychologists for the advancement of our understanding of the learning spectrum in child development. Though she was influenced initially in her early development of her method called "scientific pedagogy" by such Italian educators as Itard, Seguin, Frobel, and Pestalozzi, there is little reason to quibble with the suggestion that her brilliance was indigenous to herself and combining her own aboriginal acumen with medical school training and a university degree in psychology constituted the matrix out of which the Montessori Method evolved. Clearly crediting her early interest in learning theory to her formative years working in the Orthophrenic School in Rome, she moved beyond the institutional expectations of observation and measurement towards the creation of new and more effective materials and methodologies. Beginning with working with disabled children, mentally and physically, she soon moved to the agenda of the *Casa dei Bambini* which became the working laboratory for the experimental use of her newly created educational materials and methodologies which was in 1912 extrapolated in her now textbook classic *The Montessori Method* followed nearly 40 years later with her life's work called *The Discovery of the Child.*

The essence of her creative genius was in the realization that there is a natural tendency within every child to advance their own understanding of how things work in the world and rather than giving them an environment of controlled and sequenced learning steps the more responsive approach in fostering this independent curiosity within the child is to allow for spontaneity and environmental freedom of movement and choice. The teacher, in this world-view, becomes a facilitator of the child's own initiatives and, therefore, the responsible teacher creates a learning environment supportive of inquisitiveness, adventure, and spontaneity wherein the child sets the pace, determines the focus of attention, and the duration of that particular occupation. Within the parameters of this worldview, Montessori concentrated her attention specifically from the perspective of the young child exploring a world of opportunities rather than that of an adult looking for ways of teaching a child what the teacher wished to teach.

This acute observational skill constituted one of Montessori's great talents for it was as if she could put herself in the mind of the child and see the world from that perspective. So, for example, she redesigned the classroom furniture for children rather than using adult-size furnishings, i.e., tables and chairs accessible at the child's physical level of access and convenience. Her commonsensical emphasis upon "practical living" was paramount in her designing a free-flowing curriculum of flexibility, challenge, and excitement. Sweeping the floor and washing the dishes became a *bona fide* learning opportunity as well as tending the school's flower garden and emptying the waste paper baskets and cleaning the chalkboard erasers, not portrayed as a chore but a contribution to the community's life together. What is recognized as one of her indigenous points of brilliance was her ability to focus her attention on the children being observed. By doing so, she quickly realized the tremendous ability that even young children have of both intense concentration on that which matters to them personally as well as a robust capacity for repetitive spontaneity in the selection of activities. Children are inclined towards ordering their own learning environment when given the freedom to decide how they will spend their time and the selection of their own activities. This she eventually labeled "spontaneous discipline."

Developmental psychology, though not specifically called that at the time, constituted the core of her work in which she became increasingly fascinated with what she labeled the human tendencies in a four-tiered schema of development divided into age groups from infancy to six years of age, from six to twelve, twelve to eighteen, and from eighteen to twenty-four. There is within each stage a learning spectrum unique to that age grouping with specifically identifiable characteristics, learning modalities, and developmental imperatives crucial for a balanced learning trajectory. Of course, the Montessori Method was eventually the result of her researches and was formalized in her now classic text, *The Montessori Method*. Unlike traditional teaching models at the time which were essentially teacher-led instruction, her method was decidedly child-centered based on her scientific pedagogy. Her method was also based on an understanding of the psychology of the child in which there is an indigenous and intrinsic inclination and tendency towards the pursuit of information and knowledge relevant to the child's growing understanding of the world and its environment. Response to this natural curiosity on the part of the teacher who essentially functions as a learning facilitator to the child involves a total address to the child as a whole person physically, socially, emotionally, and cognitively. Both the International Montessori Association and the American Montessori Society list similar elements in this educational model:

a) Mixed age classrooms for children ages 2½ or 3 to 6 years old are by far the most common though older groupings exist as well.

b) Student choice of activity from within a prescribed range of options.

c) Uninterrupted blocks of work time, ideally three hours.

d) A constructivist or "discovery" model, where students learn concepts from working with materials, rather than by direct instruction.

e) Specialized educational materials developed by Montessori and her collaborators often made out of natural, aesthetic materials such as wood, rather than plastic.

f) A thoughtfully prepared environment where materials are organized by subject area, within reach of the child, and are appropriate in size.

g) Freedom of movement within the classroom.

h) A trained Montessori teacher who follows the child and is highly experienced in observing the individual child's characteristics, tendencies, innate talents and abilities.

Even before Piaget and Erikson took over the field of educational psychology with their developmental schema, Montessori was well on her way to the creation of a developmental model of incremental stages of advancement in cognitive skills as well as socially and emotionally emergent components of a well-rounded child. Being a medically trained professional who also studied the philosophy of education and developmental psychology, Montessori was no novice in understanding the complexities of human growth and development. Her schema was simple and based upon two fundamental principles, viz., the realization that children in the learning process engage in emotional and cognitive self-construction through the process of interactive experimentation with the physical and social environment, and children have an indigenous and innate capability to foster and nurture this proclivity when given the opportunity in a non-stifling setting. Healthy development in the child occurs when the child is granted freedom of movement and choice of focused interest. These innate traits or characteristics of the healthy maturing child include the following:

Abstraction, Activity, Communication, Exactness, Exploration, Manipulation (of the environment), Order, Orientation, Repetition, Self-Perfection, Work as "purposeful activity"

Montessori believed and consistently demonstrated through laboratory illustrations that these innate tendencies constitute the motivational forces controlling behavior in search of knowledge and understanding of the world and every child, when presented with this nurturing and independent learning environment, will grow at their own personal rate of maturation. More so than many subsequent developmental psychologists, Montessori was insistent upon the fundamental importance of the physical learning environment into which the child is placed. This environment should have specific characteristics which include:

- An arrangement that facilitates movement and activity
- Beauty and harmony, cleanliness of environment
- Construction in proportion to the child and her/his needs
- Limitation of materials, so that only material that supports the child's development is included
- Order
- Nature in the classroom and outside of the classroom

As noted earlier, Montessori had identified in her observations four distinct stages or what she called "planes" of development covering birth to 6 years, 6 to 12, 12 to 18, and 18 to 24 years of age, each characterized by certain developmental imperatives necessary for a productive learning environment. Let us take a moment to further explicate the details of each of these planes. By developing such operationally descriptive concepts as absorbent mind, sensitive periods, and normalization, Montessori was able to illustrate the maturation trajectory of the infant to age 6 through such behavior as raw sensorial assimilation of the physical as well as social environment such that constructing of a meaningful encounter and interpretation of the infant child's surroundings (people and places), there is an accelerated cognitive explosion of understanding occurring in what she called the absorbent mind.

This expansive cognitively robust assimilation of the child's surroundings will continue throughout childhood but will gradually commence its diminishment in terms of primacy over other developmental stages. Montessori believed that with creative imagination, a classroom could be constructed and designed specifically to both enhance and not deter this exploratory curiosity of the young child who clearly, based on careful observations, is in search of expressive modalities of environmental interaction reflected in such behavior as word play, manipulation of complex toys, a sense of orderliness in exposure to new experiences, and an intent desire to interact meaningfully with peers particularly. Referring to the innate propensities to learn as the "normalization" of psychological maturity, Montessori emphasized the central importance of both fostering and facilitating the child's own genuine sense of spontaneous inquiry and experimentation within the framework of a happy learning environment sympathetic to the child's interests and perspectives.

In the second stage of development from six to twelve, Montessori emphasized the importance of the teacher as a learning facilitator to be extremely cognizant of the developmental changes occurring in the child, emotionally, cognitively, and physically. From growth spurts to an emerging sense of the herd instinct, the child is moving increasingly towards the need for and recognition of that need for social comrades and collegial peers coupled with a clear acceleration of a sense of focused attention upon a task at hand through the effective use of one's own reasoning and imagination. Intellectual curiosity and independence of thought is merged with issues related to moral behavior towards others and loyalty to the social grouping of peers.

From 12 to 18 years of age constitute the explosions characteristic of adolescence such that heretofore interesting and even amusing physical growth occurrences such as the loss of teeth or the over-long legs is greatly outweighed in importance to the changes brought on by puberty. It is in this stage that the individual begins to take seriously issues related to fair play, honesty, and group and personal justice. There is also an equally important obsession with self-identity, who I am and what is expected of me, a sense of selfhood is emerging which demands of the individual no longer a child to come face-to-face with their own estimate of their true value to self and society with the understanding that adulthood is just around the corner with its demands and expectations, disappointments and accomplishments dependent upon one having established a viable identity worthy of respect.

The final stage of development, i.e., from 18 to 24 years of age, constitutes a somewhat under-developed period in her overall developmental psychology owing primarily to her focused attention upon the early years of growth of the child and less interest in the post-adolescent stage of maturation. Whereas Erikson will make a substantial contribution to the post-adolescent stages of development into late life and old age, Montessori rather assumed that university and marriage with the rearing of children and establishment of a career constituted the normal trajectory of most individuals and, therefore, spent little time addressing the nuances of problems which can emerge in adult life. Fortunately, Piaget and Erikson take up where Montessori seems to have left off.

Nominated six times for the Nobel Peace Prize, yet never actually receiving it, Montessori began to focus her attention on the relationship of world peace to education owing to the rise of Nazism and Fascism in Europe during the mid-1930s. Approaching old age herself, she felt it appropriate for her to redirect her creative attention to the most pressing issue of the day, namely, peace and conflict resolution. She firmly believed that her Montessori Method was uniquely designed to raise children to be peace loving and cooperative in their dealings with others and, therefore, spent the remainder of her life lecturing all over Europe and America on this topic. In short, she pointed out that a peace-based curriculum should consist of what she called "Five Great lessons" which present to the child the big picture of the world and their place in it. These Lessons include (1) the beginning of the universe and earth, (2) life comes to earth, (3) humans come to earth, (4) how writing began, and (5) how numbers began. She continued this trajectory of her contribution to developmental psychology and the education of children's philosophy of education until her death in 1952. Regrettably, a side note should end our discussion of scientific pedagogy and the tremendous contribution Maria Montessori has made to the study of children and the learning spectrum by mentioning that in 1967 a ruling by the United States Patent Trademark Trial and Appeal Board ruled that the term "Montessori" was generic and was therefore unrestricted in its use by the public so that today there is a wide scope in the use of the word Montessori such that religious fundamentalists shamelessly employ it to refer to something called the Montessori Christian Academies, etc., all to the great consternation of those who are committed to the scientific and secular nature of the Montessori Method.

List of Major Works:

The Montessori Method. New York: Frederick A. Stokes Company, 1912.

Dr. Montessori's Own Handbook. New York: Frederick A. Stokes Company, 1914

The Secret of Childhood. New York: Longmans, Green, 1936.

The Discovery of the Child. Madras: Kalkshetra Publications Press, 1948.

The Absorbent Mind. Madras: Theosophical Publishing House, 1949.

Chapter Three

Jean Piaget (1896-1980) And Genetic Epistemology

Without question, the dominant figure in developmental psychology relative to the education of children in the 20th century was the Swiss psychologist Jean Piaget, Director of the International Bureau of Education. His creative enterprise consisted not only of sustained and distinguished data-base studies of child learning but the publication and distribution of his extensive findings have been translated into dozens of languages and has had a universal impact upon the way children are understood and taught throughout the world. As Sigmund Freud created the term "psychoanalysis" to describe his discovery of methods for treating mental illness and as Viktor Frankl created the term "logotherapy" to explain what he meant by "meaning" in therapy, Piaget created the concept of "genetic epistemology" to characterize his theory relative to cognitive development in the maturation process of child education.

The effective labeling of a new concept requires the term to correctly reflect what is being explicated and such was the case with Freud's psychoanalysis and Frankl's logotherapy. Certainly this quite clearly is the case with Piaget and genetic epistemology, a term and concept which he created to explain the scope of his research as regards the pedagogical science of child education. For 25 years, from 1955 to 1980, Piaget served as Director of the International Center for Genetic Epistemology which he himself as a faculty member of the University of Geneva created following on the heels of his much earlier appointment as Director of the International Bureau of Education. The Center has so dominated pedagogical research into child cognition that as the recognized institutional leader in this field of psychological research. It isfamiliarly referenced as "Piaget's factory" owing to the extensive research and publications produced by the Center as well as an international training center for educational and psychological scholars from around the world. By the end of the 20th century Piaget was the second most referenced psychologist in the world just after B. F. Skinner but Piaget's popularity did not become dominant in the field of developmental and educational psychology until after the establishment of the Center in Geneva. Now, unquestionably, he is considered the leading pioneer in this sub-field of psychological research.

Jean Piaget was born in 1896 the oldest son of a Swiss professor of medieval literature at the University of Neuchatel, Arthur Piaget, whose mother was French, Rebecca Jackson Piaget. He grew up in the French sector of Switzerland where he early on developed a passion for biology and the study of nature such that by the age of 15 he had already published several articles in the popular magazines on mollusks. However, thanks to the encouragement of his godfather who cultivated an interest in philosophical logic and epistemology, Piaget pivoted somewhat away from natural science to a fascination with issues related to philosophy. Educated at his father's University of Neuchatel where he earned a doctorate followed by postdoctoral appointments at the University of Zurich (1918-1919) and the University of Paris (1919-1921), Piaget's precocious tendencies produced a drive to publish such that his publications following his adolescent work on mollusks were in philosophy *per se* though he also was becoming fascinated with the rise of psychoanalysis as a bona fide field of research and study.

Taking a teaching position at the Grange-Aux-Belles Street School for Boys in Paris after graduating from university, Piaget fell under the influence of the then rather distinguished educator Alfred Binet who had developed the Binet-Simon Test (subsequently labeled the Stanford-Binet Intelligence Scales). During these days of working as an assistant to Binet and marking the intelligence tests created by Binet, Piaget's attention was drawn to the fact that these children he was teaching and who were being tested consistently produced incorrect answers to specific questions such that a pattern of errors became somewhat apparent to Piaget. What occupied his attention was not so much the errors children consistently produced regarding certain questions but the substantial disparity of errors committed between younger children and older children and particularly adults. From this he quickly moved to what would become a driving force in his theory development regarding cognition. He presumed and subsequently tested an hypothesis that there is a variance in cognitive processes from one age group to another. Believing, based on his observations, that cognitive processes are distinctive to each age group as the child matures, he eventually developed a global theory of cognitive development distinguished by various levels of maturation in which at each level there are commonalities of patterned learning.

At the age of 25, Piaget left Paris and returned to Geneva to assume the directorship of the Rousseau Institute which had been under the direction of an educational psychologist and neurologist, Dr. Edouard Claparede (1873-1940), who had developed a psychological concept known as "grouping" which was essentially a variation on the trial and error modality of response in patterned human thought. He was an early member of the Zurich Freud Group and actually wrote the Preface to the first French edition of Freud's now famous *Five Lectures on Psycho-Analysis.* In 1923, Piaget married a local girl named Valentine Chatenay (1899-1983) and they had three children happily creating an ideal situation for Piaget to focus his astute observational skills on the cognitive development of his own children. Until the major professional advancement in his career in 1929 by being appointed Director of the International Bureau of Education where he remained until 1968, he served from 1925 to 1929 as a professor of psychology, sociology, and the philosophy of science at his old *alma mater* where his father had taught as well, namely, the University of Neuchatel.

Piaget's public lecturing and publications on topics related to his own research passion, cognition within child maturation, increasingly drew attention to him as a leading voice in the field of developmental and educational psychology. Just four years before he left the IBE to become Director of his own International Center for Genetic Epistomology, in 1964 he was invited to serve as Chief Consultant at conferences on cognition and educational development at Cornell University and the University of California at Berkeley. These two conferences focused upon the relationship between cognitive research and curriculum development within the public schools of America. His presence and contribution at these two conferences were reflective of his international reputation gained during his teaching years at both the University of Geneva and the University of Paris. He would eventually in 1979 receive the Balzan Prize for Social and Political Sciences followed in 1980 by his death and burial with his deceased wife in an unmarked grave in the Cemetery of Kings in Geneva which was at his own personal request.

Piaget's educational and intellectual development carried him over a wide terrain of research interests which might be divided into four general categories of focus, viz., his psychological interest in developmental models of learning, the biological focus on intellectual development, the extension of this model of developmental intellect, and finally his crowning accomplishments in the study of cognition and figurative thought patterns in the developing mind of the child. Let us explore these four stages of Piaget's developing interests before explicating a detailed assessment of his overall concept of genetic epistemology. In the early 20s he became enamored, owing somewhat to the birth of his own children, in the development and cognitive functioning of the child's mind noting the movement, suggested by Freud and the psychoanalytic practitioners of the day, from clearly an egocentric narcissism to a socio-cultural interest which Montessori would have highlighted in her own earlier work. By combining both his psychological training and expertise with the clinical methodology he had developed during particularly his postdoctoral studies in Zurich and Paris, he created a research tool that would serve him substantially over the coming years which he called the semi-clinical interview employed in the direct engagement with children being observed. By alternating and balancing a series of both standardized and non-standardized questions posed to the children being interviewed, he pointed out that what he was watching for was a demonstration of spontaneous conviction based on the unpredictability by the child of the anticipated questions' content. Discovering, as he explained it, that there was from the interviewees an incremental and gradual development and movement from merely intuitive responses to increasingly scientific and socially acceptable responses. Piaget hypothesized that the motivation of the child was conditioned and dictated by the social interaction involving the younger children feeling that their ideas were being challenged by the older children whose responses were perceived by the younger children as more sophisticated and intellectual. Piaget's employment of this technique was used on the famous Australian psychologist Elton Mayo which constituted the foundation for what became known as the famous Hawthorne Experiments, a reactive research tool developed by Henry Landsberger. Piaget's efforts in these regards resulted in his receiving an honorary doctorate from Harvard University in 1936.

Returning to his childhood fascination with biological research, Piaget turned his attention to the study of the process of thinking and its intellectual development in which he began to hypothesize that the interaction between thinking and development could have a biological component suggestive of the evolution of the human species for survival. These adaptive processes he called assimilation and accommodation, the first process records the child's responsiveness to new events and episodes in its life which is perceived to have an enduring consistency of occurrence whereas the latter process involves the child taking the initiative to alter or modify an identified sequencing of events so as to make an entirely new event or episode resulting in the formation of a new procedural mechanism. Convinced from his own laboratory observations, he suggested that the young infant is engaged in the process of what he had defined as assimilation when they sucked their thumb as well as everything around them upon which they could lay their hands believing that the infant essentially converts all available objects into objects for sucking. This process was simply a conversion formula indicating the child's own mental structures so that Piaget concluded that the process of transforming objects in the world to conform to the child's own needs essentially constitutes assimilation.

Beyond mere assimilation, however, the developing child not only converts all available objects within reach to meet their own individual needs (such as for sucking), they also and inevitably engage in the altering or modifying of objects (what he called mental structures) to conform to the demands and expectations of the child's immediate environment. This constituted for Piaget an illustration of the second fundamental process, viz., accommodation. Commencing as a newborn infant by engaging in basic reflexive actions such as sucking, the child rather quickly begins handling and manipulating extraneous objects available for access as items for sucking. By making this transition of the objectification of objects there is the transition from the act of the assimilation of available objects to the necessary modification and alternation of external objects such that the initial reflexive response of sucking gives way to the reflexive action of grasping and holding external objects. This shift or transition from response to action constitutes what Piaget thought of as intellectual development for the balancing of these two processes stimulates intellectual growth.

From psycho-social to biological to logical models of intellectual development, Piaget demonstrated a Renaissance interest and capacity in the study of child cognitive processes. Contending based on his clinical studies and laboratory observations that intelligence itself develops incrementally in a series of identifiable stages which are linked in their maturity to the age of the child and are necessarily progressive and positively developmental in nature such that each stage must be met and conquered before the next stage can be mastered (not unlike Maslow's contention that the hierarchy of needs must be met in ordered sequence with no jumping ahead of needs not yet met). Piaget felt the same regarding these developmental stages for, he suggested, every child creates a view of the world and reality reflective of each particular developmental stage relevant to the age of the child. As the child moves ahead rising through the various stages of intellectual development, this occurs by virtue of the child bringing along what has been already learned and assimilated to the next level requiring a continual reconstruction of reality based on new data, concepts, and thought patterns. This upward trajectory of intellectual development is predicated upon the child's continuing ability to bring forward what has already been learned with what is being learned and yet to be learned such that a continual reconstruction of reality is occurring reflective of intellectual growth and development, a metaphor of upward and onward in the race for intellectual maturity.

A distinguishing feature of what we now recognize as Piaget's genius was his inclination to study what would eventually be called "figurative thought," that is to say, those functional features of the intellect such as perception and memory which are not strictly speaking logical and sequential in formation or recollection. Whereas terms and concepts which are by their very construction logical in composition are necessarily by definition reversible because there is an identified beginning and ending with sequential steps connecting start to finish. The attractive feature of logical thought is the predictability of process, beginning with an hypothesis and working through to the end and then working it backwards to the originating hypothesis. This balanced symmetry constitutes what is recognized as logical reason. Though Piaget fully understood how logical thought worked, he realized through careful observation that the young child does not proceed on the basis of logic but rather the use of figurative thought modalities which are not systemic.

Piaget realized when studying the young child that the perceptual concepts of interest to him evidenced in the thought patterns of the young were not subject to sequential configurations based on logical progressions. He found that the use of illustrative materials, photos, pictures, images were helpful in explaining what he meant by the figurative process of non-logical thought. Like pictures which cannot have their various components sorted or extracted from the total are not unlike memory which is not totally recallable and never reversible as with logical thought but rather constituted a collage of impressionistic manifestations. A profoundly important recognition of the development of the child's mind had to do with Piaget's early realization that biological maturation is linked to the emerging capability of logical and sequential thinking and that there is a notion of "readiness" which is crucial in the learning process. Information can only be assimilated in relationship to the biological readiness of the child's mental capabilities so Piaget argued that young children should not be expected to grasp realistically the meaning and application of concepts and theories until they have matured sufficiently to appropriate such understanding.

Cognitive development, therefore, Piaget suggested must be allowed to progress along its own biological stages and that to rush the learning process by insisting that a young child's mind should and could grasp sequential logical thought before they are mature enough to understand progression and construction of systems is a common mistake. He went so far in his later years to refuse to come to America any longer to share his research owing to the fact, as he explained it, that the Americans no matter what I show them we have learned about child development and their learning spectrum always ask, "Can we do it faster?" Speed is not the goal; comprehension and understanding are the goals in child development.

More so than with Maria Montessori, Piaget was a research scientist first and a practical technician second whereas Montessori was a hands-on practitioner. Though she held university appointments throughout her career, they were also praxis oriented, laboratory and illustrative work, dealing with children in a classroom observational setting from which she then developed her handbooks on "how to get the job done." Piaget, though quite interested in the application of his findings, was primarily a research scientist attempting to understand cognitive development in the mind of the young child and to develop theories of explanation of that complex functioning of the brain which led him to call his approach "genetic epistemology." Whereas Montessori defined herself first and foremost as a teacher, Piaget preferred to call himself an epistemologist interested in an understanding of the fundamental mechanism involved in the development of knowledge in the young child. Naturally, the observational laboratory was central to his research methodology but his focus was upon the cognitive structures involved in knowledge development recognized as a component of biological operations within the mind of the child. His structural and cognitive approach to the theory of the learning spectrum eventually became the dominant school of thought in developmental psychology and educational theory.

As noted earlier, Piaget's two fundamental concepts in his theory of cognitive development within the young child involved assimilation and accommodation, but emphasized concurrently the relevance of biological interaction with cognitive processes. Though criticized by members of the biological community specializing in genetic research, Piaget contended that his use of the term genetic was appropriate as it is applied to the relationship of child maturation to both cognitive development and biological parameters and nothing in either intellectual development or biological maturation in the child occurs outside the central importance of genetics. Through observational studies in the laboratory of children and adolescents Piaget was eager to emphasize the fact that genetic epistemology was designed to address issues related to the search for the fundamental foundations of variegated differences in knowledge levels related to cognitive and biological maturation of the child over time tracked through four developmental stages which he explicated in all of his work. These four stages are (1) sensorimotor stage, (2) preoperational stage, (3) concrete operational stage, and (4) formal operational stage. Let us explore these in some detail as they are central to the Piaget system of cognitive development.

The first of the four stages of cognitive development in the child Piaget chose to label the "sensorimotor stage" which covers birth to about age two during which time the crucial experience of movement and activity on the part of the infant precipitates a gradual awareness of the child's own body and its senses, particularly of touch, smell, and sound. The fundamental orientation of the infant is upon itself, a natural narcissism, such that they have yet to interact with the physical and social environment from any perspective but their own egocentric interest or what Freud would reference as the dominance of the libido and provocation of the id. Within this initial stage of sense exploration, Piaget identified six sub-levels of developmental cognition.

(1) Simple reflexes from birth to one month old at which time infants use reflexes such as rooting and sucking.

(2) First habits and primary circular reactions from one month to four months old during which time infants learn to coordinate sensation and two types of

schema (habit and circular reactions). A primary circular reaction is when the infant tries to reproduce an event that happened by accident (ex.: sucking thumb).

(3) Secondary circular reactions from four to eight months old at which time children become aware of things beyond their own body; they are more object-oriented. At this time they might accidentally shake a rattle and continue to do it for sake of satisfaction.

(4) Coordination of secondary circular reactions from eight months to twelve months old during which time children begin to do things intentionally. They can now combine and recombine schemata and try to reach a goal (ex.: use a stick to reach something). They also begin to understand object permanence in the later months and early into the next stage learning thereby that objects continue to exist even when they can't see them.

(5) Tertiary circular reactions, novelty, and curiosity from twelve months old to eighteen months old during which time infants explore new possibilities of objects; they try different things to get different results.

(6) Internalization of schemata.

After the initial cognitive emersion experience of the infant, the "preoperational stage" from about age two up to age seven sees the coming of an intense interest in verbal communication used to engage both the social environment of people as well as the physical acquaintance with the naming of things. Though Piaget pointed out that at this point the young child is not able to grasp the experiential concept of logical reality and being devoid yet of the capacity to engage reflectively upon the possible management and control of information and things in the environment including people, the young child does accelerate an interest in and capacity for play and pretense. Still unable to see the world as others see it, i.e., not able yet to transcend an egocentrically dominated purview, the fundamentally important cognitive development of self-play and interactive play during which time there is experimentation with manual handling and manipulation of items in the environment without cognizance of these items' purposes or functions. Still functioning at the symbolic mode of concept consideration, notions of play are restricted to self-interest activities without yet the interactive capacity for corporate sharing, what Piaget chose to label the pre-operational stage of cognitive development.

Though still dysfunctional in terms of a viable grasp of logical processes, the young child at this pre-operational stage is beginning to grasp and even configure stable concepts including magical beliefs such that the young child during this stage is particularly vulnerable and susceptible to religious instruction. Operational performances still elude the young child's physical as well as mental capabilities though imagining the doing of a thing is more likely than the actual ability to do them such that the idea precedes the deed thus causing children at this stage to imagine an episode or deed without actually accomplishing it. Still unable to see the world as others see it owing to the continued dominance of an egocentric orientation of the young child's mental development, Piaget felt and demonstrated in his laboratory researches that the young child has developed both a symbolic functional purview as well as an intuitive thought process. These two developing couplets in intellectual growth are crucial for a well-rounded cognitive address to the demands of the encroaching world of people and things. The symbolic function is indicated when the child demonstrates the ability to understand, represent, remember, and picture objects and people in its mind's eye without actually having those images immediately present in the child's purview. On the other hand, the intuitive thought process is indicated when the child reaches the cognitive maturity to initiate questions of "why?" and "how come?" indicating a primordial quest for knowledge and information relative to the impinging world around them of people and things.

These two stages of symbolic function and intuitive thought are broken down into two sub-stages of development. The gradually developing capacity to employ symbols to represent the child's understanding of the physical and social environment constitutes the symbolic function stage of development. A classic demonstration of this symbolic development is when this age child draws pictures of the family realizing as the child does that the images are not to scale but the significance is in their being represented artistically and, therefore, symbolically as well. Piaget believed that between the ages of four and seven, the commencement of the formulation questions reflecting the child's growing curiosity about the world and the people and things in it suggest the gradual emergence of intuitive thought processes. An initial and pristinely naïve effort at logical reasoning suggests sequencing cognition of descriptive explanations offered in response to the inquisitiveness of the child. Realizing as the child does, reflected in the questions being asked, that the child is in possession of a great deal of information which it is attempting to sort and label for sequential and therefore logical understanding, Piaget has characterized this cognitive development as suggestive of this preoperative thought involving centration, conservation, irreversibility, class inclusion, and transitive inference, each reflective of intellectual growth.

The exponential jump in cognitive development occurs, according to Piaget, in the "concrete operational stage" such that from about age seven to eleven the child has begun to develop logical cognitive skills by which Piaget meant that the child is learning how to understand reversibility and, therefore, logical progression. Limited understandability in terms of physical capabilities and with a gradual diminishment of egocentric narcissism, the child now has the opportunity of cultivating the effective use of understanding the world and people and things in it from a logical and conservational perspective, that is, reasonably sequential and retainable over time. The final stage of cognitive development according to Piaget is what he has chosen to label "formal operational stage" in which there is clear evidence of the development of the capacity for abstract thought and logical reasoning such that the retention of what has been thought in the abstract becomes a great continuing source of cognitive development. Conserving or retaining what has been thought in the abstract and applied in the physical world of people and things constitutes the defining characteristic of formal operational thought but not only can the child now think logically and abstractly but can use that knowledge for intentionality of movement addressing problem-solving strategies and the multiplicity of tasks simultaneously.

The theory of cognitive development within the Piaget schema is suggestive of a gradual progression in the development of the intellect of the child from the moment of birth through adolescence. Piaget built his developmental model based on laboratory observations and experiments conducted primarily at his research Center at the University of Geneva, and this model has dominated both educational as well as developmental psychology theory throughout most of the 20th century and well into the 21st century. The attractive feature of this Piaget Model is its common sense simplicity based on observations in which any trained individual and the particularly attentive parent can engage. The new infant begins immediately to be actively motivated by sounds and senses focusing early on specific sounds, particularly the mother's voice, and items which pass before it coupling these observations with the experimentation related to hand, arm, feet, and leg movements which the child gradually brings under control over time. Being possessed of a libidinal drive to self-satisfaction, the young child begins to develop a sense of me/not-me such that the differentiation between other people and external objects become a progressive self-reflecting abstraction and by learning to distinguish sounds and sights, people and objects, there develops an empirical abstraction producing an ability to differentiate between people and items as well as to begin to understand that items in the world of people and things endure even when out of sight or not present. This Piaget called the cognitive stage of development. By having learned both to identify and to differentiate between items, objects, things and people, the child gradually develops a capacity to create greater and more complex compositions of items and things resulting in an increasing sophistication of interaction with the outside world. This perpetual reorganization of constructed concepts constitutes the central core of cognitive development.

Intuitively, one would think that these stages, as in Maslow's model of hierarchy of needs or Erikson's stages of development, would be sequential and incrementally predictable but such is not the case as clinical and laboratory research has found. Developmental progression we have learned from Piaget and his colleagues' research at the

Center is sporadic, erratic, and variable in terms of sequencing and progression owing to the now recognized fact that new learning is necessarily linked to that which is already known. Therefore, when a child is confronted with or encounters something new and different the grasping of it is linked to him having already a context within which to place this new experience, insight, or object. Understandably, the learning spectrum is then connected to what is already known such that the incremental and progressive nature of learning is not smoothly transitional from one level to another but can be quick and speedy or slow and plodding depending on the depth of the contextual framework within which this new experience is situated. And, it must be pointed out that instead of this learning process being all consuming in terms of seeking and accumulating new knowledge rather the child spends a significant amount of time manipulating and re-configuring new insights into the matrix already well developed. Cognitive development is necessarily a contextualization of that which is already known with that which has just been encountered as new and in need of categorization.

Rather than a smooth progression from unknown to known, this process of cognitive development Piaget has taught us is necessarily dialectical in nature such that each new level or stage of cognitive refinement and expansion is based upon the child learner's efforts at differentiation, integration, and synthesis of new insights into the established one. Understandingly, therefore, the learning is sequential in that new materials must be contextualized within already known information as building blocks are stacked in a pattern of supportive development rather than merely thrown together randomly. This logic and reason play a major role and the progression in learning is necessarily linked to the child's cognitive developments related to logical thinking and reasoning. Coming when they did and not just what they were, Piaget's new insights into the cognitive development of children introduced the educational and psychological world of child studies to both insights into how knowledge is actually accrued through maturation but also the presentation of new understandings of the learning process itself. The capacity for the acceleration of accumulation and assimilation of increasingly complex structures of knowledge is now understood to be an incremental gathering, sorting, and linking of that which is newly learned to that which has already been grasped. The knowledge platform of the developing mind of the child provides the matrix within which the complexification of materials is sorted into an understandable and reasonable assemblage of related and contingent items, objects, and ideas. This process, though not smoothly incremental, is inevitably the mechanism whereby the inevitable complexification of information-related configurations can occur with refinements allowing for elaboration of insights into each bit of new materials building upon each as each expands exponentially, metaphorically like a nuclear reaction.

An added feature of this cognitive complexification of information sorting and manipulation is the discovery that there are actually rules of governance of information gathered so that life is not characterized by mere happenstance or chaos but events. The proliferation of materials needing to be learned and understood fall within a spectrum of logical relatedness such that prediction and anticipation of response is both commonplace and reliable. Piaget suggested that, for instance, in the developing of an ethical and moral awareness of behavioral expectations that the process of objectification, reflection, and abstraction becomes crucial in the weighing of decisions informed by moral and ethical insights requiring action that is both effective as well as justifiable. The discovery by Piaget at his research Center of the young child's ability to discriminate much earlier than formally thought possible but also that the logical capacity for cognitive operations characterizes the youngster's mind more pervasively than originally imagined. Surprisingly absent and disappointing as well is the realization that Piaget's experiments in the cognitive development of the young child verified and validated much of what Maria Montessori was saying and demonstrating pragmatically in her own schools which were promoting her scientific pedagogy all the while Piaget was continuing to illustrate similar understandings of the child's capacity to learn with his genetic epistemology.

Piaget's insightful genius in the field of epistemology had to do with his belief that he could actually explain how knowledge is accrued in the human mind by focusing upon what he called "sociogenesis" and the gradual accrual of insights accumulated and assimilated into a growing matrix of logically connected bits of information. The fabric of the mind's logical configuration provided an arena for the expansion of both the materials gathered through experiential exposure to the unknown collapsed into the known but also the logical extrapolation of this growing composite to an ever-expanding world of knowledge. By studying children, how they think and act based upon careful observation, it is possible for the scientific and educational communities to come to a deeper biological and psychological understanding of just how knowledge is accumulated and how it grows in the human mind, a real understanding of genetic epistemology.

Within this context and somewhat under the influence of the philosopher Emmanuel Kant's concept of empirical categories, Piaget developed three intellectual constructs or what he referred to as "schema," viz., *the*

behavioral, the symbolic, and the operational schemata.
The behavioral schemata is essentially an organized pattern of behaviors which are employed to represent and respond to objects and experiences in the child's purview of life. The symbolic schemata involves internal mental images and symbols both seen and heard which the individual uses to illustrate and express their experiential encounter with the world. The operational schemata is increasingly sophisticated in that it is the manifestation of the internal mental workings of the child's mind illustrative of how the child grasps and manipulates ideas and thought systems into a logical pattern of continuity and reasonableness for understanding.

As Piaget had consistently emphasized, we see that children use both the processes of assimilation and accommodation in the development of these schemata or cognitive frameworks for the purpose or function of perceptual insight and the interpretation of the nature and meaning of new experiences, open to every sensorial encounter with a drive to collect and collate new information into the already established matrix of things known. The human drive illustrated in the child's receptivity to new experiences is a demonstrably complex and time-consuming enterprise which characterizes the child's agenda on the learning spectrum of cognitive development. Little wonder, Piaget is quick to point out, that the child is always busy making demands upon the physical and social environment in order to continue this accelerating accrual of new data. In short, the three schemata developed by Piaget consist of four fundamental characteristics, viz., they are critically important building blocks of conceptual development, consistent process of modification and manipulation, on-going experiential modifications of the new materials, and a generalized grasped of that which is experienced as new based on both experience and previously accumulated insights.

Piaget was eager to emphasize that the *behavioral, the symbolic, and the operational schemata* were in a constant mode of revisions, elaborations, alternations, and expansions directly related to the on-going experiential adventures and explorations of the inquisitive and curious child. Through the process of the cognitive construction of reality in the child's growing mind the child's knowledge base continues to develop and grow exponentially with an added propensity to confront dilemmas and solve complex problems. Developmentally, this is enhanced and facilitated through the growing function of logic and reason in the child's repertoire of cognitive capabilities. The brain, Piaget explains based on his insights gained in genetic epistemology, is unceasingly engaged in restructuring its understandings of the world based upon the continuation of the influx of new insights, experiences, and understandings which it must receive, adapt, modify, reconfigure, and categorize within the already existing cognitive structures having been developed and put in place from previous learning experiences. In a post-Piaget world, the relevance of biologically relevant insights being gained from DNA research continue to advance our understanding of how the brain develops physically and how the mind develops cognitively but, alas, Piaget was not privy to what is now being learned about these biological processes relevant to our understanding of both the development of the brain physically and the mind cognitively.

Today Piaget is still considered the most important developmental psychologist of all times owing to his pioneering innovations in research methodology and the development of the theory of learning called genetic epistemology. He aspired to revolutionize the way research was being conducted relative to the learning spectrum of child development and he was joined in this quest by such leading figures as Montessori, Erikson, and Anna Freud. Yet it was Piaget who established the Center at the University of Geneva and it was Piaget who continued to refine a theory of learning which has yet to be surpassed in importance. Moving quickly from the employment of traditional research methods of observation and data gathering, he was eager to develop more sophisticated methods based on an elevated sense of responsiveness to the needs of the child being observed rather than dictated insights set by the research community, a child-oriented phenomenology of research rather than a scientist-oriented agenda.

Early on Piaget was among the first to employ psychometrics and psychiatric clinical examinations as two new methods of research seeking empirically pure data unadulterated by bias and prejudices based on philosophical speculations rather than laboratory researches using empirically collected data from observation and experimentation. The study of child thought processes was an occupying obsession with Piaget early in his career and the interest and fascination of how children accumulate, sort, and integrate new information into existing matrices always proved dominant in his research motivations. Initially enamored with Freud and psychoanalytic insights into the workings of the unconscious mind, Piaget eventually moved away from this approach owing to what he considered to be a deficiency in empirical rigor. This shift in his orientation resulted in a distancing of genetic epistemology as a school of thought from the psychoanalytic community but endeared Piaget to the more empirically-oriented psychological, educational, and medical communities.

It was Piaget's conviction, based on his own laboratory work, that the use of speech itself was significantly different in children from adults. He attempted to demonstrate the differences in the use and meaningfulness of language between children and adults through a laboratory experiment with children in the telling and interpretation of particular stories known to adults as well as children. After listening to a particular story, the child was asked to re-tell the story to a child friend in his own words rather than reciting the storyteller's words. The research focus was upon the nuancing of word usage suggestive of what the child heard from what was actually said, a distinction between the child's word choice and that of the adult storyteller's word choice. Variations in word choices between the child and the adult are suggestive, Piaget contended, of both the child's naturalistic understanding and interpretative reasoning through the employment of alternative and more familiar words conveying in the child's mind the same sense of the story. He was and is acclaimed to be the dominant pioneer in this field of child linguistics and is valued for his introducing the importance of examining children's conversations within a social context of conversation between adults and children.

The problem, of course, with psychometrics and other similar tests was the difficulty of determining whether or not the child being tested was either sincere or pretending based on the child's understanding of and expectations relative to the testing process itself. Piaget was fully cognizant of this danger. Based on extensive use of this methodology and judging from the experience of its variability and volatility, Piaget began to explore other methods of research which he himself developed, what he thought of as a "clinical" method of research. With this approach, he would interview a child with a series of questions and then systematically examine in detail the responses in an attempt to track the reasoning operation within the child's mind as the child processed the questions. Using their responses, he then attempted to assess the worldview of the child as suggested in the responses during which time he focused his attention on the child's spontaneity in responding. Becoming unsatisfied with the scripted nature of the interview process itself, he shifted his attention and focus to a more natural environment in which the child is presented with a problem of some sort and was asked to sort out a solution without adult assistance. The motivation for Piaget through the continued process of exploring and experimenting with different research modalities was to get at the way in which a child's mind works, how the child thinks through a situation, a problem, a challenging dilemma such that a satisfactory solution is finally reached. He believed he could make such a discovery.

Sounding very much like the Montessori Method, in Piaget's work he became convinced that education must be child-centered rather than teacher-centered, it must focus on the freedom of intellectual exploration and aboriginal intention to construct a reality based on data gathered and assimilated by the child doing the learning. Self-understanding of the learning environment constituted the fundamental building blocks for a responsive educational environment for children. The essence of Piaget's theory of learning called attention to the disadvantages of the teacher-centered approach for that approach discounted or overlooked the original impetus of learning in the first place, i.e., the natural curiosity of the child's mind, the desire to learn as an indigenous characteristics of the human child. Rather than enforcing instruction by the teacher, the child's own freedom of exploration and curiosity constitutes the most effective pedagogical style according to the findings of

Piaget. His quest was centered around the concept of knowledge, what it is and how one gets it. Knowledge as understood by Piaget constituted the ability to modify, transform, and manipulate an object or idea in such a manner as to allow of the understanding of it to be integrated into the already existing matrix of knowledge within the child's mind. The result of this assimilation and accommodation is increasing knowledge. The cognitive development of the child's mind is connected to a learning spectrum linked to the experiential encounter with that which is unknown or new and its interfacing with that which is known and familiar. This process involved logical reflection and active participation in the exploration of the new and its relationship with the familiar thereby integrating new and old into a new construction of reality based on the unending accrual of that which is unknown merged with that which is known. Sometimes called scaffolding or building-block construction, this process constitutes the increase in knowledge at every level and age of maturation such that the learning spectrum is essentially the result of a transformation process of knowledge accrual.

We cannot conclude our study of Piaget without acknowledging his great contribution to the study of moral development in children. Piaget believed in two fundamental principles regarding moral education, viz., children develop the understanding of moral behavior in incremental stages of maturity and they are actively engaged in the creation of a worldview based on their understanding and encounter with the world of reality. This creativity in constructing a worldview also involves and implies the creation of a moral code based on their perception and integration of moral behavior from their encounter with the social environment in which they are maturing. Embodying the moral code of those who are observed within the social matrix of the growing child constitutes the basis for the development of a personal moral code within each child. Freud called this the social inculcation of conscience and the inevitable appearance of the super-ego. Piaget's famous 1932 book titled *The Moral Judgment of the Child* constitutes one of the major contributions to the understanding of moral development in children in the 20th century. His philosophical foundation was built upon a tripartite constructed definition of morality as universalizable, generalizable, and obligatory coupled with his refusal to equate cultural norms to moral norms thereby distinguishing his understanding of moral development from that of Freud and aligning himself essentially with the Kantian theory of universal imperatives. Piaget believed and attempted to illustrate demonstrably through clinical and laboratory texts that morality as such among children is created from within the matrix of peer pressure and norms rather than that of a mandated authoritarian system of imposed rules of behavior. Piaget's theory places much more weight on the influence of the child's peers than parents when it comes to the development of such things as a sense of equality, reciprocity, and justice.

Because of the centrality of peers within the life of a child wherein ethical norms and moral behavior are cultivated, Piaget placed a heavy emphasis upon the psycho-social processes operative with interpersonal interaction such that a key differentiation must be acknowledged between types of relationships. For example, Piaget explains that asymmetrical relationships are those in which one interacting participant holds more power over that relationship than does the other individual such that mutual awareness of this domination by one over the other implies a fixed and inflexible connection, called by Piaget social transmission. This may characterize the parent/child relationship as well as occasions of either charismatic dominance or bullying.

On the other hand, a symmetrical relationship exists where a cooperative sharing of power is equally distributed between participants in the social matrix wherein genuinely beneficial and authentic instances of intellectual sharing and exchange naturally occur with each participant enjoying the freedom of expression without fear of censorship. This is the environment within which real learning occurs where the child's mental processes are not restricted by a dominant force but rather the child is free to reconstruct information conducive to his increasing learning capacity and content of knowledge. This learning experience is characterized by flexibility and is regulated by the rules of logic and reasoning rather than an external authority source. Finally, for Piaget, the key distinction between cultural norms and moral judgement is that the former originates in the asymmetrical world of authoritarian domination whereas moral judgement emerges naturally in an environment of cooperative relationships of an egalitarian confluence of peers.

From Montessori's scientific pedagogy to Piaget's genetic epistemology is not a great leap but one of significance. Whereas the former grew out of a pragmatic interest in the teaching of the young and the development of creatively supportive learning materials and the learning environment *per se*, the latter grew out of an academic focus upon the theory and philosophy of cognitive development in children and the desire to understand scientifically how knowledge is gained and grows in the child's mind. The former was praxis-based application of indigenous insights by a compassionate teacher and the latter was a theory-based inquiry by a trained research psychologist. Piaget set a standard of scientific research methodology which elevated the value of his findings to a new and higher level of understanding of the cognitive functions of the maturing mind of the child. Combining a biological interest in brain development with a psychological interest in the development of the mind, Piaget brought to the forum of child studies a two-fold level of profoundly important insights which are still today being valued and their implications explored and extrapolated.

List of Major Works (English translations only)

The Language and Thought of the Child (London: Routledge & Kegan Paul, 1926)

The Child's Conception of the World (London: Routledge and Kegan Paul, 1928)

The Moral Judgment of the Child (London: Kegan Paul, Trench, Trubner and Co., 1932)

The Origins of Intelligence in Children (New York: International University Press, 1952)

The Psychology of Intelligence (London: Routledge and Kegan Paul, 1951)

The Child's Construction of Reality (London: Routledge and Kegan Paul, 1955)

The Early Growth of Logic in the Child (London: Routledge and Kegan Paul, 1964)

Genetic Epistemology (New York: W.W. Norton, 1971)

The Principles of Genetic Epistemology (New York: Basic Books, 1972)

Science of education and the psychology of the child (New York: Orion Press, 1970)

The Grasp of Consciousness: Action and Concept in the Young Child (London: Routledge and Kegan Paul, 1977)

Psychology and Epistemology: Towards a Theory of Knowledge (Harmondsworth: Penguin, 1972)

Chapter Four

Erik Erikson (1902 – 1994) and Stages of Development

When a newly emerging theory of human development combines with a creative imagination in the form of a person, there is reason to believe that something significant is about to happen. Such is the case with a most unlikely candidate for greatness, namely, Erik Erikson. The ferment with both the educational and the psychological communities at the beginning of the 20th century relative to new insights into the nature of human development and the relevance of that understanding to the education of children was tremendous. Not only because of the great contribution Marie Montessori was making in the study of the actual praxis of education in the development of her scientific pedagogy but also in the work of Jean Piaget who greatly elevated the scientific study of knowledge acquirement and cognitive development in his emerging theory of genetic epistemology. All the while this was going on in educational laboratories throughout Europe and the U.S., there was a comparable explosion of theory building based on laboratory research in the field of child psychopathology led by Anna Freud's application of psychoanalysis to the study of child mental illness. She was joined in England by Melanie Klein and in the U.S. by Karen Horney. The confluence of these pedagogical and psychopathological experiments and insights is epitomized in the life's work of Erik Erikson who studied with Anna Freud as well as Marie Montessori and whose contribution to developmental psychology set a new and higher standard of theory and practice.

Erik Homburger (Erikson) was born on the 25th of June, 1902, in Frankfurt-am-Main in Germany and died in Harwick, Massachusetts, on May 12, 1994. His mother was a young woman named Karla Abrahamsen from a prominent Jewish family in Copenhagen and his natural father, a Dane named Erik Salomonsen, deserted his mother before Erik was born. At the time of his birth, his mother was "officially" married to a Jewish stockbroker and at his birth, he was registered as Erik Salomonsen. She later trained as a nurse in Karlsruhe and in 1904 married a Jewish physician named Dr. Theodor Homburger who was, at the time, serving as Erik's own pediatrician. In 1909, Erik Salomonsen became Erik Homburger and in 1911 he was officially adopted by his stepfather. Personal identity was an obsession with Erik throughout his childhood and adolescence for at the temple school the children teased him for being "Nordic," owing to his blonde hair and blue eyes, and at public school he was teased for being a Jew.

Upon Erik's eventual arrival in America as his adopted homeland, having fled Germany with the rise of Nazi proliferation, he changed his surname to Erikson when he took U.S. citizenship. Personal, racial, and religious identify seemed to have plagued Erickson from his earliest memories and haunted him throughout his childhood, adolescent, and adult life. It has been suggested that possibly this life experience itself was a significant ingredient in leading him to the development of his now famous eight stages of development.

Following public school in Germany where his first love was quite clearly art, Erikson studied at a variety of places in Munich and Florence and eventually arrived at the door of what was then still a newly emerging discipline in psychology, namely, psychoanalysis. It should be pointed out here that Erikson did not ever pursue formalized educational training beyond the high school diploma, relying rather upon his own confidence and insights into the field of which he was most interested. He did attend a "humanistic gymnasium" in Karlsruhe, Germany, where he was not a particularly good student while, nevertheless, did quite good work in ancient history and art as his records show. Refusing to heed his step-father's urgings to pursue medicine, Erikson left home to travel across central Europe and within the next year enrolled in an art school and, for a brief time, accepted the fact that even an aspiring artist could learn something in an educational setting.

Becoming restless yet again, he left that school and set out for Munich to study at the famous art school, the Dunst-Akademia. Two years there, he then moved to Florence while generally wandering aimlessly around Italy "soaking up sunshine and visiting art galleries." He later would write that he finally came to realize that "such narcissism obviously could be a young person's downfall unless he found an overweening idea and the stamina to work for it."

In 1927 at the age of twenty-five, Erikson took up a teaching post at an experimental school for wealthy American children living with their parents in Vienna. This school, called the Kinderseminar, was founded to serve the needs of American professionals studying in Vienna to become psychoanalysts and was under the directorship of a psychoanalyst, Dorothy Burlingham, who was the daughter of the internationally acclaimed New York jeweler, Charles Tiffany. She was herself a professionally trained psychoanalyst and not reluctant to promote this school of thought to all with whom she came in contact. Needless to say, the young Erikson fell under her spell from whom not only did he study and learn as well as undergo psychoanalysis but also was introduced to the Montessori education method and to Anna Freud herself, a lifelong collaborative friend of Dorothy Burlingham. Erikson also and quite naturally was introduced to and welcomed into the Vienna Psychoanalytic Society which was Sigmund Freud's center of teaching and training psychoanalysis to medical professionals and selected layman alike. Besides undergoing psychoanalysis at the hands of Anna Freud herself, Erikson also took the Certificate from the Maria Montessori Teachers Association in Vienna, his only academic credential throughout his whole professional life.

Naturally, young man Erikson was greatly influenced by these heady relationships and professional experiences which, undoubtedly, were instrumental in fostering his passion for analytical studies of childhood maturation. From a modest teaching appointment, Erikson managed to squeeze out an incredibly provocative life experience which led to his now famous ideas and theories about human personality development. In 1929, he married Joan Serson, an American teacher and dancer who was at the time a member of Anna Freud's and Dorothy Burlingham's experimental school in Vienna where Erikson himself taught. By 1933, they had two sons and the whole Erikson family then attempted to emmigrate to Copenhagen where he had hoped to secure citizenship based upon his natural father's nationality. He had hoped to establish a psychoanalytic practice there, little known in Denmark at the time, but the effort failed and they were forced to look elsewhere to begin again, having feared Hitler's rise to power. That same year he completed a course of study at the Vienna Psychoanalytic Institute.

His enthusiasm for this general field of work and study eventually led him to emmigrate to the U.S. in 1933 where he was, quite fortuitously, provided study and teaching opportunities at some of America's most distinguished centers of learning including Harvard, Yale, and the University of California at Berkeley. Upon his arrival in Boston in 1933, he set up as one of the very few child psychoanalysts in the country and carried out research on children at the prestigious Harvard Psychological Clinic where he enjoyed a close friendship and working relationship with both Henry Murray and Kurt Lewin. From 1933 to 1935, he enjoyed an appointment as a clinical and academic Research Fellow in Psychology in the Department of Neuropsychiatry at Harvard Medical School. He momentarily enrolled in a Ph.D. in psychology at Harvard but quickly, within months, withdrew never again to make such an attempt. From 1936 to 1939, he served under an appointment in the Department of Psychiatry in the Institute of Human Relations at the Yale University Medical School where he thoroughly enjoyed continuing his work and interest in personality development and cross-cultural studies.

Erikson's early work concentrated primarily upon psychological testing with special attention to the ways and means of extending Freudian psychoanalytic theories in relation to the effect of social and cultural factors upon human development and personality. He was particularly fascinated with the impact of these insights upon how society affects childhood and development. Because of his driving interest in multi-cultural studies of childhood and society, he became a great student of cultural anthropology, especially as relates to the study of children and personality development cross-culturally. As with Abraham Maslow, the works of Margaret Mead and Ruth Benedict proved pivotal to his own conceptual framework and subsequent theoretical development in this area. To further deepen his understanding of cross-culturalism and child development, he journeyed to the Native American communities of the Oglala Lakota (Sioux) and the Yurok peoples where he stayed for an extended time of observations and interviews. The richness of these experiences fed his ambitions in theory and conceptual development while also demonstrating to him some of the apparent deficiencies of Freudian theory as relates to personality development. This encounter with psychoanalytic shortcomings coupled with the richness of his cross-cultural experiences eventually led to his development of what came to be called the "biopsychosocial" perspective on childhood and society.

Eventually migrating with his family to the University of California at Berkeley in 1939, he continued his concentrated efforts in the study of child welfare and personality development and practiced as a clinical psychologist at the San Francisco Veterans Hospital where he treated trauma and mental illness. By 1942, Erikson had risen to the position of professor of psychology at the University of California at Berkeley where he enjoyed assisting Jean MacFarlane in the Child Guidance Study. During the McCarthy era, he moved back to Massachusetts from whence he had come owing to his refusal to sign a loyalty oath which was now being required of all teachers in the State of California. In 1951, he joined a group of mental health professionals at the Austen Riggs Center in Stockbridge, Massachusetts, which was a private residential treatment center for mentally ill young people. He also, and amazingly, continued to maintain a part-time teaching appointment at the Western Psychiatric Institute in Pittsburgh, Pennsylvania while also teaching at the University of Pittsburgh and the Massachusetts Institute of Technology.

From 1951-1960, he taught and worked in New England, but in the summer of 1960, he spent a year at the Center for Advanced Studies of the Behavioral Sciences at Palo Alto, California, and was the next year rewarded by being invited to teach at Harvard University. Erikson retired in 1970 from his clinical practice but not from his busy schedule of research and writing. He died in Harwick, Massachusetts, on May 12, 1994 and was followed three years later by his Canadian wife, Joan, whom he had met and married while still living and teaching in Vienna. She was herself an academic and particularly fascinated with the study of childhood development and became a major collaborated with Erikson in his research and publications. They had two sons, one of whom was institutionalized as an infant with Down Syndrome, and a daughter. The experience of having a Down Syndrome child almost wrecked their marriage and the pain and suffering, denial and prevarications, to say nothing of the physical and psychological distancing of themselves from this child, Neil, scared the parents and quite decidedly the other children as well.

Most biographers do the disservice of failing to mention Neil Erikson in their biographical sketches of Erikson to the detriment of both Down Syndrome research and the Eriksons alike. Neil was institutionalized from the hospital as a newborn and his siblings were simply told that he died at birth. Later on, the older son was told of Neil's birth and that he was still alive living in an institution but the other children remained in the dark until Neil's death. Joan visited him infrequently and later Neil was permanently institutionalized in a prestigious public hospital for mentally retarded children. No photos of Neil were ever taken. At forty-one years of age at the time of Neil's birth, Joan blamed herself and was eaten up by the guilt. The marriage suffered severely as Erik continually attempted to close out the reality of Neil's life. When the Eriksons were moving back to New England, they told their other children of their seven year old brother, Neil, and that he was to be left behind in California. None of the children had ever seen him. The experience of leaving a little brother behind as they moved away frightened the daughter profoundly and parental trust suffered severely as a result. Neil lived to be twenty-two years old and died in 1965 while Erik and Joan were in Europe. They called their oldest son and daughter who were now living back in California and asked them to arrange for the burial of Neil. Neither parent returned for the funeral or internment of his ashes.

A prolific writer, it has been suggested that all research and publication subsequent to Erikson's first and indisputably his most famous book in 1950, *Childhood and Society*, was merely a continuing commentary on that book. He continued to push his interest in the life cycle (eight stages of development) during which time he introduced the concept of the "identity crisis" within adolescence. A gradual movement away from psychoanalytic theory and practice was seen as he moved closer to the Third Force and humanistic interests within psychological research and writing. This shift was reflected in his subsequent books such as *Young Man Luther* (1958), *Identity and the Life Cycle* (1959), *Insight and Responsibility* (1964), *Identity: Youth and Crisis* (1968), and *Gandhi's Truth* (1970) which won for him the Pulitzer Prize. In 1974, he published *Dimensions of a New Identity*, and with the editorial revisions made by Joan Erikson, his 1982 book, *The Life Cycle Completed: A Review*, was republished in 1996 which happily extended the stages of old age within the life cycle model, thus completing Erikson's contribution to developmental psychology.

Many distinguished scholars have established themselves on the strength of one great book such as Frankl and Adler and Rogers, while others wrote and wrote and wrote, leaving behind a library of research and scholarship such as Freud and Jung and Maslow. It can be argued that Erikson's name and reputation was established and secured with the publication of his first book in 1950, *Childhood and Society*. Erikson's fascination with the study of children, their personality development and their maturation, resulted in the writing of his most famous text. Here, he elaborated his approach of "triple bookkeeping," as he called it, namely, that understanding a person or behavior involves taking into account somatic factors, social context, and ego development, each in relation to the other. To unpack the somatic aspect of child development, Erikson developed and helpfully expanded Freud's theory of psychosexual development. Erikson chose to explore the power of social context in relation to child-rearing practices and their effects on later personality through some fascinating anthropological and psychoanalytical analysis of the Native Americans, particularly the Sioux and the Yurok cultures.

Though trained by Anna Freud and within the psychoanalytic tradition of Freudian analysis, Erikson was not disinclined to move in his own sphere of thought just as he had chosen not to pursue a traditional university education. Erikson looked at ego development in particular through an analysis of the significance and role of "play," for it was in child's play that he was able to emphasize the need for integration. These three processes, somatic, social, and ego development, are interdependent and that each is both relevant and relative to the other two. This was quite decidedly an advance over traditional Freudian concepts of personality development and child sexuality.

Before we go further in our appreciative assessment of this classic text, let us simply here recite the primary contributions to the understanding of child development which Erikson has brought to the table of psychological insight. First, he elaborated and modified the theory of psychosexual development as produced by Freud; second, he drew from his own clinical experience in working with ego development among children for his theory construction; and third, he employed anthropological data to emphasize the significance of the social context for child rearing and cultural process for personality development.

A fundamental component of Erikson's theory of ego development is the assumption that the development of the person is marked by a series of stages that are universal to humanity. This was, of course, a very bold claim. The process whereby these stages evolve, he explains, is governed by the "epigenetic principle" of maturation. By this Erikson (1950) explains: "(1) that the human personality in principle develops according to steps predetermined in the growing person's readiness to be driven toward, to be aware of, and to interact with, a widening social radius; and (2) that society, in principle, tends to be so constituted as to meet and invite this succession of potentialities for interaction and attempts to safeguard and to encourage the proper rate and the proper sequence of their enfolding."

In his great classic, Erikson outlines a sequence of eight separate stages of psychosocial ego development, commonly called "the eight stages of man." Far from the speculative mysticism of Jung and his genetically inherited "archetypes," Erikson is keen to postulate that these stages are the result of the epigenetic unfolding of a "ground plan" of personality that is genetically transmitted, and this is a "universal phenomenon." By epigenetic (*epi* means "upon" and *genetic* means "emergence"), Erikson has proposed a concept of development which mirrors the notion that each stage in the life cycle has an optimal time, i.e., "critical period," in which it is dominant and hence emerges, and that when all of the stages have matured according to plan, a fully functioning personality comes into existence.

Going further, Erikson is eager to emphasize that each psychosocial stage is accompanied by a "crisis," that is, a critical turning point in the individual's life that arises from physiological maturation and social demands made upon the person at that stage. The various components of personality are, in his theory, determined by the manner in which each of these crises is resolved. Conflict is a vital and integral part of Erikson's theory, because growth and an expanding interpersonal radius are associated with increased vulnerability of the ego functions at each stage. However, it is important to keep in mind that, according to Erikson, each crisis connotes "not a threat of catastrophe but a turning point and, therefore, the ontogenetic source of generational strength and maladjustment."

In a review of Erikson's *Childhood and Society* over fifty years ago, the now famous Dr. Eric Berne wrote a critically appreciative assessment of Erikson's book for the *New York Times*. We will quote extensively from that review to give an idea of the impact Erikson was having on the psychological profession at the time. Berne himself was becoming established as a major force for what he called "transactional analysis." He was extremely complimentary of Erikson's pioneer spirit in the study and treatment of children as relates to psychoanalytic understanding of ego development. Erikson, Berne points out, early emphasized the importance of early frustrations in the development of adult anxieties and actions, believing that while sexual conflict was at the basis of most neuroticism in Freud, the main reason for emotional disturbances in America today lies in the lack of "an emotional integration." This harps back to emotional immaturity caused by a prolonged period of childhood and to certain unique characteristics of American culture and family training. Erikson, of course, and due to his study of cross-cultural childrearing practices, was very cognizant of the fact that personality development is deeply imbedded in the social mores of the child's own culture. This constituted the fundamental starting point of Erikson's monumental work, *Childhood and Society.* In the next section, we will consider some of the major conceptual frameworks and theoretical constructs which were presented in Erikson's entire corpus of research on personality development.

Without doubt, Erikson (1966) was one of the leading 20th century psychologists working in the area of personality development, what he called the "psychosocial growth of the ego." Interestingly and not particularly to his credit nor benefit, Erikson always insisted that he was not a creative thinker but rather a commentator and, possibly, an elaborator of the psychoanalytic theories of personality development introduced by Freud. He claimed simply to have complimented Freud's work with further investigations of sociological, anthropological, and biological data relevant to personality. In spite of his protestations to the contrary, there are four distinct areas in which Erikson moved away from and beyond Freudian psychoanalytic theory of personality.

First, Erikson shifted the emphasis from the prominence of the id in Freudian theory to the ego which Erikson believed to be the center and basis of human behavior. Called "ego psychology," this shift proposed an understanding of the ego as an "autonomous structure of personality" which follows a course of social-adaptive development that is distinct from but parallels the id and the instincts. Second, Erikson distinguished himself with his emphasis upon the child's relationship to parents and the socio-historical matrix within family life in which each child's ego develops, for good or ill. Third, Erikson's ego development theory covers the entire span of psychological growth and development throughout the individual's life. Freud's theory was woefully brief after adolescence. Finally, there was a great divide between Freud and Erikson when it comes to the nature and resolution of psychosexual conflicts within an individual's life. Whereas Freud wished to resolve these issues by delving into the unconscious reservoirs of the adult through dream analysis and word association, Erikson wished to focus upon the adult's capacity to move forward by assessing life situations and embracing a mode of operation designed to foster healthy living.

The fundamental ingredient in Erikson's theory of ego development is the assumption that the development of the individual is marked by a series of "stages" that are universal to every person throughout the world. The process whereby these stages evolve is governed by the fundamental principle of maturation, what he called the "epigenetic" principle. He explained that this concept means "(1) that the human personality in principle develops according to steps predetermined in the growing person's readiness to be driven toward, to be aware of, and to interact with, a widening social radius; and (2) that society, in principle, tends to be so constituted as to meet and invite this succession of potentialities for interaction and attempts to safeguard and to encourage the proper rate and the proper sequence of their enfolding."

In his highly acclaimed, *Childhood and Society,* Erikson identified and extensively elaborated upon a sequence of eight separate stages of psychosocial ego development, what were usually in shorthand fashion referred to as the "eight stages of man." These eight stages he carefully identified, in his clinical practice and in his laboratory research, as the epigenetic unfolding of a "ground plan" of personality that is genetically transmitted. Whereas Jung would have us believe that archetypes are genetically transmitted, Erikson is keen for us to see that the stages of life are genetically transmitted throughout the human species. The fully matured human person arrives on the scene when each of these eight stages have been allowed to mature and function in their own time within the personality of each individual. However, it must be pointed out that Erikson was also eager for us to understand that each stage of development carries with it a "crisis," that is, a critical turning point in the individual's life that arises from physiological maturation and social demands made upon the person at that stage. Each component of the individual's personality develops in relationship to the method in which and the success with which each crisis is met and handled. Conflict, in Erikson's psychosocial theory of development, is crucial and indispensable for healthy development of the ego in each person.

For Erikson, the psychosocial stages of ego development were chronologically sequenced and each was companioned with a "crisis" component which could work either positively or negatively. Though accused of being "too mechanistic" in his developmental stages, he was insistent throughout his career that these stages were, indeed, sequential, and most definitely universal to the human animal. We will discuss briefly each stage of psychosocial development and its corollary crisis.

Corresponding only somewhat to Freud's "oral stage" of infant development, Erikson's first stage (Infancy) placed "trust" and "mistrust" in juxtaposition to each other with the psychosocial strength gained by the individual to be that of "hope." He believed that a sense of trust was essentially the cornerstone of a healthy personality. This sense is sometimes thought of as "confidence," and it grows out of an infant's "inner certainty" about the world as a safe, stable place and people as nurturing and reliable. It all stems from the infant's earliest experiences with mother and feeding rituals.

The first major psychological crisis for the child wherein mistrust emerges is related to the quality of maternal care which is unreliable, inadequate, and rejecting, thus fostering a psychosocial attitude of fear, suspicion, and apprehension in the infant. Erikson believed that the development of a healthy personality is not just based on the rise of trust versus mistrust in the infant's earliest maternal experiences but rather of the dominance of trust over mistrust. The psychosocial strength gained from this successful management of trust over mistrust, says he, is the emergence of "hope" in the child's attitudes towards the future and his social relations with others.

By a year and a half, the child is ready to move to the stage of "autonomy versus shame and doubt" and the personality skill to be learned here is that of "will power." As the child gains in neuromuscular maturation, verbalization, and social discrimination, he begins to explore and interact with his environment more independently and the parents are, therefore, confronted with decisions regarding balancing "holding on" with "letting go." The meeting and handling of this psychosocial crisis, both for the child who wants to "let me do it" and the parent who wants to "let me help you," will set in motion wheels of positive or negative development which not only will encourage or stifle autonomy and shame but will both inculcate a sense of "will power" while affecting the earliest stage of life's sense of trust and mistrust. Each stage of ego development is linked to the previous one and a kind of building block phenomenon occurs such that strong ego boosters grow while weak ego boosters stifle personal development. Failure to inculcate and nurture a sense of autonomy in the child, Erikson believes, will instill in the child a sense of shame, something Erikson believes to be akin to "rage turned upon himself" because he has not been allowed to exercise his personal freedom. Shame grows in the personality when autonomy is stifled and, thereby leads to the curtailment of a responsive feeding of the child's "will power." Erikson (1950) goes on to say: "Will power is the unbroken determination to exercise free choice as well as self-restraint in spite of the unavoidable experience of shame, doubt, and a certain rage over being controlled by others. Good will is rooted in the judiciousness of parents guided by their respect for the spirit of the law." Parental guidance at this stage must be firm, Erikson says, but protective of that sense of trust achieved during the previous oral stage. He continues, "Firmness must protect him against the potential anarchy of his as yet untrained sense of discrimination, his inability to hold on and to let go with discretion. As his environment encourages him to 'stand on his own feet,' it must protect him against meaningless and arbitrary experiences of shame and of early doubt."

From trust to autonomy to a sense of "initiative" is the developmental process of the four to five year old child. The resolution of the conflict between initiative and guilt is the final psychosocial experience in the preschool child's personality development, during what Erikson calls the "play age" of childhood from about four years old to the beginning of formal schooling. This resolution of conflict versus guilt produces in the child a deep sense of purpose or, if unresolved, the loss of direction and purpose towards the future. "Initiative," explains Erikson, "adds to autonomy the quality of undertaking, planning, and 'attacking' a task for the sake of being on the move, where before self-will, more often than not, inspired acts of defiance or, at any rate, protested independence."

At this time, a child begins to experience the feeling of

being a person who actually counts, one who thinks for himself, "I am what I will be." The balancing of this sense of initiative with the experience of guilt is very much dependent upon how parents handle this last pre-school developmental stage in the child's life. Successful development of this sense of initiative produces what Erikson calls a "goal-directedness" in the child. "The child begins to envisage goals for which his locomotion and cognition have prepared him. The child also begins to think of being big and to identify with people whose work or whose personality he can understand and appreciate. 'Purpose' involves this whole complex of elements." A sense of guilt, on the other hand, is fostered by parents who employ excessive amounts of punishment (verbal or physical) in response to the child's urge to love and be loved. The child's future potential to work productively and achieve self-sufficiency within the context of his or her society's economic system depends markedly upon the ability to master this psychosocial crisis of "purpose" produced by the initiative versus guilt dialectic.

At stage four, the school age years, the child moves to another major level of ego development and personality. This "school age" period covers the years between about six and eleven and in classical psychoanalysis is referred to as the "latency period." Here, industry versus inferiority appears and the crisis produced by this tension is that of a sense of competency. We have now moved, in the positively developed personality, from trust to autonomy and initiative to industry or, contrariwise, for the negatively developing personality of the child from mistrust, shame, and guilt to a sense of inferiority. Hope, will power, and purpose as character traits developed in response to the psychosocial crises of each developmental stage now give rise to what Erikson calls a sense of competency on the part of the healthy child. Erikson has summarized these developmental stages as a movement from "*I am what I am given*" to "*I am what I will*" to "*I am what I can imagine I will be*" to, now at the fourth stage, "*I am what I learn*." "In school," Erikson (1950) explains, "with varying abruptness, play is transformed into work, game into competition and cooperation, and the freedom of imagination into the duty to perform with full attention to the techniques which make imagination communicable, accountable, and applicable to defined tasks." Learning, demonstrating, moving forward in one's capacity to perform, to compete, and to demonstrate ability is now in full sway. The danger at this stage, of course, lies in the potential of failure which will inculcate a sense of inferiority or incompetence. The child's sense of competency and industry is, in modern society, primarily affected by and determined by his educational successes. Yet, cautions Erikson (1968), a genuine sense of industry involves more than simply one's educational achievements and occupational aspirations for it also includes a feeling of being interpersonally competent, the confidence, if you will, that one can exert positive influence on the social world in quest of meaningful individual and social goals. This fundamental strength, namely, competency, is the basis for participation in the social, economic, and political order of one's culture and society.

The fifth stage of ego development falls between childhood and adulthood and is a pivotal period in the development of the individual. Adolescence is that period in a person's development where "ego identity" and "role confusion" come face to face with the resulting psychosocial crisis of "fidelity." This stage in Erikson's developmental scenario is the most-well developed in his overall schema. Erikson (1978) elaborates on the nature of "ego identity." "The growing and developing youths, faced with this physiological revolution within them, are now primarily concerned with attempts at consolidating their social roles. They are sometimes morbidly, often curiously, preoccupied with what they appear to be in the eyes of others as compared with what they feel they are and with the question of how to connect the earlier cultivated roles and skills with the ideal prototypes of the day ... The sense of ego identity, then, is the accrued confidence that one's ability to maintain inner sameness and continuity (one's ego in the psychological sense) is matched by the sameness and continuity of one's meaning for others." Three fundamental elements characterize ego identity. First, individuals must perceive themselves as having inner sameness and continuity. They are the same person over all. Second, the individual's social *milieu* must also perceive a sameness and continuity in the individual, so group affirmation is crucial. Third, the adolescent must have gathered confidence in the relationship between his world and that of his social group by having a sense of who he is and having that affirmed by others. However, when this mutuality of ego identity affirmation is absent, adolescents will encounter what Erikson calls "role confusion." In the absence of a personal identity which is strong enough to see a youngster through these developmental years, an identity crisis is inevitable. This crisis is most often characterized by an inability to select a career or pursue further education with the added deficit of a deep sense of futility, personal disorganization, and aimlessness. The feeling of inadequacy, depersonalization, alienation, and even a negative identity may result. When the adolescent has confronted the challenge and ego identity has finally emerged sound and operational, "fidelity" emerges and this, says Erikson (1966), refers to the individual's "ability to sustain loyalties freely pledged in spite of the inevitable contradictions of value systems." Being true to one's own ego identity while remaining loyal to the social matrix within which that ego identity has developed and emerged is a characteristic of fidelity and prepares the adolescent for the next stage of development.

By virtue of a well-established ego identity characterized by fidelity or loyalty to oneself and one's social *milieu*, the individual, says Erikson (1975), is now "ready for intimacy, that is, the capacity to commit himself to concrete affiliations and partnerships and to develop ethical strength to abide by such commitments, even though they may call for significant sacrifices and compromises." This is the stage in which courtship, marriage, and early family life come on the scene. By "intimacy," Erikson has in mind the sense of intimacy most of us share with a spouse, friends, brothers and sisters, and parents or other relatives. He also, however, speaks of intimacy with oneself, that is, the ability to "fuse your identity with somebody else's without fear that you're going to lose something yourself." This two pronged sense of intimacy is crucial in a well-developed relationship -- intimacy with others within the framework of intimacy with oneself. The inevitable danger in this developing sense of intimacy is, of course, a sense of isolation where neither intimacy nor social involvement are possible or productive.

The inability to enter into positive and intimate personal relationships leads the individual to feelings of social emptiness and isolation. Merely formalized and superficial social relationships are inadequate to meet the developmental needs of these individuals, however, and given the fact that they may be suffering from an over dependence upon self-absorbing behavior to relieve their sense of loneliness, they drift further and further away from realistic opportunities to experience and nurture feelings of intimacy. Their behavior, then, becomes inevitably counterproductive. The psychosocial strength being sought here and the one which is realized in the healthy development of a sense of intimacy is that of love. In addition to its romantic and erotic qualities, Erikson regards love as the ability to commit oneself to others and to abide by such commitments, even though they may require self-denial and compromise. "Love," explains Erikson, "is mutuality of devotion forever subduing the antagonisms inherent in divided function."

The "middle years" of an individual's stages of life are fraught with prospects of creative activity or degenerative stifling. What is not possible is for nothing to happen to the individual's ego development and psychosocial maturation. This process continues throughout life, it does not stop for age and only ends with death. The countervailing options for the middle age adult is either what Erikson calls "generativity" or "stagnation" and the psychosocial crisis produced is that of "care."

"Generativity" occurs, says Erikson, when an individual begins to show concern not only for the welfare of the next generation but also for the nature of the society in which that generation will live and work. This developmental stage in life has to do with the willingness, or not, of the individual to meet the challenge of assuming responsibility for the continuation and betterment of whatever is instrumental to the maintenance and enhancement of the society in which the individual lives. It represents the older generation's concern in establishing and guiding those who will replace them. Failure to assume this responsibility, to assert oneself into the mainstream of social betterment and improvement leads to individual and societal stagnation. The sense that one does not wish to be involved, not participate in teaching the next generation the values necessary for successful and fulfilled living, all lead to a failure of courage and a

111

diminishment of one's social worth and the worth of society at large. Those in their middle years who embrace and nurture generativity will produce a sense of "care" needed for the ongoing contribution to the improving quality of life for the next generation. Individuals lacking generativity cease to function as productive members of society, live only to satisfy their needs, and are interpersonally impoverished. This is often called the "crisis of middle age" where the person has a sense of hopelessness and tends to feel that life is meaningless. Caring for oneself, for others, for society at large is the benefit and reward to those who develop and nurture a sense of contribution to the wider society.

The "mature years" constitutes the last stage in life's journey. Every culture has this stage well developed according to its own social values, history, and composition. It is a time when the individual's ego is confronted with the option of "integrity" or "despair" and the crisis which comes with this confrontation can lead to a general sense of "wisdom" about life and how to live it. "Only in him who in some way has taken care of things and people," says Erikson (1986), "and who has adapted himself to the triumphs and disappointments adherent to being, the originator of others or the generator of products and ideas -- only in him may gradually ripen the fruit of these seven stages -- I know no better word for it than ego integrity." With the inevitable demands brought on by these declining years of the need to adjust to deterioration of physical strength and health, to retirement and reduced income, to the death of a spouse and close friends, and the need to establish new affiliations with one's age group, there is a marked demand for shifting one's attention from a focus upon future life to that of one's past life.

The sharing of past experiences, of days gone by, with those who are younger characterize this stage in life and often, depending on the culture, is perceived by the listeners and observers of these older persons as a sense of "wisdom," a kind of helpful knowledge about what is important and how to live a meaningful and fulfilled life. "The wisdom of old age," explains Erikson, "involves an awareness of the relativity of all knowledge acquired in one lifetime in one historical period. Wisdom is a detached and yet active concern with life in the face of death." On the other hand, the lack or loss of ego integration in older individuals is earmarked by a hidden dread of death, a feeling of irrevocable failure, and an incessant preoccupation with what might have been." "Fate," he explains, "is not accepted as the frame of life, death not as its finite boundary. Despair indicates that time is too short for alternate roads to integrity: this is why the old try to doctor their memories." Ego integration leads to a sense of real and practical wisdom worthy to be shared with the young and in that process the individual comes to a deeper sense of self-fulfillment and contentment with life as he has lived it with hope for the future.

Though a trained and never rebellious psychoanalyst in the true Freudian school of thought, Erikson, however, never ceased to claim allegiance to Freud while boldly asserting the further development and contribution of his thought to the Freudian school of psychotherapy. His psychosocial theory of personality development relied upon a strong argument for the centrality of ego psychology, developmental changes throughout the life cycle, and an understanding of personality against the background of social and historical forces. Contrary to Freud, Erikson held that the ego was an autonomous personality structure and he concentrated his efforts, therefore, upon ego qualities that emerge during the fundamental stages of maturation.

Erikson argued that the ego continued its development throughout life and identified eight stages in which that development occurs. These psychosocial stages characterize the human life cycle, as he called it, and he contended that the individual's personality is determined by the resolutions of the conflicts which emerge in each of these developmental stages. His theory is, of course, rooted in his basic assumptions concerning human nature itself, namely, (1) a strong commitment to the assumptions of holism and environmentalism, and (2) a moderate commitment to the assumptions of determinism, rationality, objectivity, pro-activity, heterostasis, and knowability.

Though some have registered concern over the relationship between the personal life of Erikson, his family life and his failure to come to both an emotional and professional embracing of the life of his mentally retarded child, and the profundity of his thought, most psychotherapists today are, however, indebted to Erikson for calling attention to the eight stages of the life cycle. Granted, they are mechanistic, sometimes even antiseptic, they have, nevertheless, spawned a whole new way of viewing human maturation and have nurtured a deeper appreciation for what a modified psychoanalytic theory of personality can still offer to the modern practice of psychotherapy.

Though not the only psychologist to develop stages of development, Erikson clearly represents one of the great minds of the 20th century in the carefully constructed and systemic approach to the study of the maturation process from infancy to old age. Other schools of thought in psychotherapy have made tremendously important contributions to the study of personality development for without Sigmund Freud's initial inquiry into the stages of development, i.e., oral, anal, genital stages, it is difficult to imagine how the further schools of theory such as Maslow's hierarchy of needs or the work of Carl Jung, Viktor Frankl, and Carl Rogers could have appeared to say nothing of the innovative insights of Horney, Klein, and certainly of Anna Freud. Yet, it seems clear that Erikson's Eight Stages of Development in the life cycle has set a standard and an agenda for all subsequent theorists and researchers in developmental psychology for the coming century. Though subject to refinement, development, and theoretical advancement to be sure, Erikson has clearly provided the scientific community with a foundation upon which much can be built.

List of Major Works:

Childhood and Society (1950)

Young Man Luther: A Study in Psychoanalysis and History (1958)

Insight and Responsibility (1966)

Identity: Youth and Crisis (1968)

Gandhi's Truth: On the Origins of Militant Nonviolence (1969)

Life History and the Historical Moment (1975)

Adulthood (edited book, 1978)

Vital Involvement in Old Age (with J. M. Erikson and H. Kivnick, 1986)

The Life Cycle Completed (with J. M. Erikson, 1987)

CONCLUSION

Where do we go from here?

Lamentable is the fact that these three distinguished research scholars did not have a more lively and creative opportunity to collaborate in their work such that there is reason to believe that they were either unaware of the others' contributions to their shared field of interest or they chose to ignore them. All were clearly influenced by Sigmund Freud and each in their own way were directly in communication with Freud during their formative years of theory building. The challenge and question confronting the educational and psychological communities of researchers and scholars today is how now to move ahead in the broad field of developmental psychology particularly as the focus on the child has been elevated to a national agenda both in university research laboratories and in government sponsorship. The tripartite foundation comprised of Montessori's *scientific pedagogy*, Piaget's *genetic epistemology*, and Erikson's *eight stages of development* in the life cycle of the human person certainly constitutes a solid basis for confidence in our capacity to develop theories and practices which are measurably effective. No one will question the central importance of Montessori, Piaget, and Erikson in our understanding of the *learning spectrum in child development* and with confidence in what they have provided for researchers, teachers, and psychologists. We have every reason to believe that the future is fraught with great promise of ever-increasing insights into the complexities of human consciousness and our capacity to expand and deepen our knowledge of ourselves and the world in which we live.

GLOSSARY OF TERMS IN DEVELOPMENTAL PSYCHOLOGY

(selected and modified from the Psychologenie.com website)

Abductive Reasoning   A process through which a person tries to show the connection between unrelated facts and uses his intuitive thinking power for the same.

Abnormal Psychology   A branch of psychology that deals with the disorders/deviations or the abnormal behavior of the mind. It is a broad subject and covers the study of depression, obsession, compulsion, sexual deviation, etc. The experts, who are associated with the study of this field are the psychotherapists, clinical psychologists, and counselors.

Abnormality   A behavioral attribute that reflects the deviation of mind from its normal state or typical behavior.

Abreaction   A psychoanalytical term related to the activity of reliving an experience to clear or purge the emotional baggage associated with it is called abreaction.

Aboulia   A situation in which the subject is unable to make decisions or take an initiative. Earlier, aboulia was known as the Blocq's disease.

Acceptance and Commitment Therapy   Aimed at increasing the psychological flexibility of a person. It is a branch of cognitive-behavioral therapy, and is a kind of psychological intervention based on observational, experimental, and experiential information collection methods.

Acting Out   The term used for an action that is performed, going by the impulsive behavior, rather than constructively responding to a particular situation.

Actualization   Term used in reference with self-actualization is defined as the process of realizing one's potential. The term is used to explain various theories of psychology and according to Abraham Maslow, actualization is the final stage of psychological development that is reached, after all the basic and mental needs of an individual are fulfilled.

Attention-deficit/Hyperactivity Disorder   A disorder commonly diagnosed in children, and is characterized by hyperactivity and attention problems. ADHD is the abbreviated form of attention deficit hyperactivity disorder, and around 3-5% children are affected by this problem globally.

Adjustment Disorder   A disorder, in which, an individual is unable to make the necessary adjustments required to fulfill the needs and to overcome the stress related problems.

Affect   The feeling or experience that is associated with an emotion.

Affectional Bond   Term used for the attachment between two individuals displayed through their behavior. The term was coined by John Bowlby, and it underwent development during the period between 1940s and 1970s.

Aggression   Behavior which incorporates the intention of causing harm or pain to another individual.

Agitated Depression   A state of mind which exhibits the symptoms of depression and mania simultaneously.

Agitation   State of restlessness or excitement of emotions. The extreme form of this agitation is psychomotor agitation.

Agnosia   The state in which an individual is unable to identify or recognize persons, objects, shapes, sounds or smells.

Akathasia   A state or condition in which an individual is unable to remain still or motionless.

Alcohol Amnestic Disorder   Alcohol amnestic disorder is caused by the deficiency of thiamine (vitamine B_1) and the symptoms of this disorder include retrograde amnesia, anterogade amnesia, confabulation, apathy and lack of insight. Also known as Korsakoff's syndrome.

Alcoholism   Compulsive alcohol consumption and the loss of the ability to recognize its adverse effects.

Alexia   Used to denote the acquired form called dyslexia in which the person suffering from this problem loses his ability to read.

Alexithymia   The person suffering from this disorder loses his capability of understanding and conveying emotions.

Alienation
The process of disintegration of the perceptual and cognitive

powers of the mind is termed as alienation.

Allophilia   Positive feelings felt for people despite being from different race, religion, nationality, class, gender, etc.

Alogia   The condition in which a person is unable to speak fluently.

Alzheimer's Disease   A degenerative disease in which the patient suffers from a long term decline in the cognitive functions. Memory loss associated with difficulty to remember the facts that have been learned recently are the common symptoms of the Alzheimer's disease. In the further or advanced stages of the disease, the patient becomes irritable, aggressive and faces mood swings.

Amnesia   Term used for memory loss or the disturbance in the memory.

Anal-retentive   A type of personality or behavior in which a person is obsessed with or gives extra importance to the details.

Anal Stage   The phase in the life of a child between 1 to 2 years of age associated with toilet training.

Analysand   The term given to a patient (or client) being treated psychoanalytically.

Analytical Psychology   A branch of psychology, proposed by a psychiatrist from Switzerland, Carl Jung known as Jungian psychology.

Anorexia Nervosa   A disorder in which the person suffers from the fear of gaining weight. Anorexia nervosa is a psychiatric illness, in which the person doesn't gain weight and his body image too, is distorted.

Anterograde Amnesia   Loss of the ability to create or form memories with the occurrence of the event that caused amnesia.

Anti-social Behavior   A type of behavior which shows no consideration for others and lack of judgment. Anti-social behavior of an individual might cause damage to the property of others. Such kind of behavior is the manifestation of the anti-social personality disorder.

Antilocution   Verbal remarks that are used against a person or community without addressing them directly to the target. The term can be understood perfectly with the help of the phrase, 'talking behind someone's back'.

Antipathy   The opposite of sympathy.

Anxiety   An unpleasant feeling which is associated with fear, uneasiness or worry is termed as anxiety. It is a psychological state characterized by emotional, cognitive, behavioral and somatic components.

Anxiety Disorder   An umbrella term used to cover the different types of anxieties and fears that were included in psychiatry at the end of the 19th century.
Apathy   A state in which a person suppresses his emotions like motivation, excitement, concern, passion.

Aphanisis   The loss of sexual desire.

Applied Behavior Analysis   Application of

behavioral principles that are derived from experiments for bringing about an improvement in the socially significant behavior is termed as application behavior analysis.

Assertiveness   A personality trait characterized by the behavior of communicating without being afraid to speak one's mind. Assertive people are known to defend their personal boundaries without being aggressive or passive.

Atkinson-Shiffrin Model   A psychological model that proposes the structure of memory. As per the Atkinson-Shiffrin model, there are three sequential stages of human memory called the short-term memory, long-term memory and sensory memory.

Attachment Theory   Concerned with the study of relationships between human beings from the psychological, ethological and evolutionary perspectives is termed as attachment theory.

Attachment Disorder   A person's inability to develop a bond or attachment with the 'primary care giving figures' in his stages of childhood is termed as attachment disorder.

Attribution   Refers to the manner in which an individual describes or explains the cause of events, his own behavior and also the behavior of others associated with the events.

Attributional Bias   Cognitive bias that affects the process of decision making as to what or who is responsible for a particular cause of events is termed as attributional bias.

Atypical Depression   A disorder which is characterized by mood reactivity. A person with this disorder experiences improved mood in response to positive events.

Authoritarian Personality   Characterized by the traits such as authoritarian submission, conventionalism, authoritarian aggression, superstition, power, stereotypy, destructiveness, toughness, cynicism and exaggerated concerns over sexuality is called authoritarian personality.

Autism   Characterized by impaired communication and social interaction is termed as autism. Repetitive and restricted behavior are some of the other symptoms found in people with this disorder.

Autism Diagnostic Observation Schedule   The standardized protocol used for the assessment of communicative and social behavior associated with autism.

Aversion Therapy   Therapy in which a stimulus is provided to the patient while simultaneously being exposed to a form of discomfort. The aversion therapy conditions the mind of the patient in such a manner that the stimulus is associated with the discomfort caused. The treatment is used to stop certain undesirable behavior.

Avoidant Personality Disorder   A disorder in which a person exhibits characteristics like social inhibition, sensitivity to negative evaluation and feeling of inadequacy. People suffering from this disorder tend to avoid social interaction.

Avolition   A state in which a person lacks the desire, motivation or drive that is required to pursue a meaningful goal.

Barnes Akathisia Scale   A rating scale used in the assessment of the severity of drug-induced akathisia.

Barnes Maze   A tool used for the measurement of memory and spatial learning in psychological laboratory experiments.

Beck's Cognitive Triad   A triad which involves negative thoughts about the self, world and the future is termed as Beck's cognitive triad.

Behavior Modification   The improvement in behavior which is brought about by the implementation of behavior change techniques that are demonstrated empirically.

Behavior Therapy   A form of psychotherapy which is used in the treatment of anxiety disorders, depression, and phobias is known as behavior therapy.

Behavioral Imprinting   Learning during which an individual learns rapidly and which is independent of behavioral consequences is termed as behavioral imprinting or just imprinting.

Behavioral Psychology   A branch of psychology which is based on the proposition that thinking, feeling and all the other actions performed by an individual are different forms of his behavior.

Behavioral Science   Deals with the exploration of different activities of living organisms and the interactions that takes place between them is termed as behavioral science.

Bias Disorder   A disorder in which an individual is inclined towards violence and believes that war is the ultimate solution to problems is defined as bias disorder.

Bibliomania   The habit of collecting books excessively. The problem might result into the person damaging his health and social relations.

Bipolar Disorder   A person suffers from episodes of elevated mood and depression subject to extreme conditions such as mania (elevated mood) and depression, the problem is termed as bipolar disorder.

Catalepsy   A nervous condition which causes the muscles to go rigid and the posture fixed. This condition or state is characterized by loss of sensitivity to pain.

Cataplexy   A rare disease found in 5 out 10,000 people which results into the affected person losing muscle tone. People with narcolepsy are prone to this problem which is often triggered by emotions and associated with Excessive Daytime Sleepiness (EDS).

Catatonia   A syndrome that is associated with motoric and psychic disturbances such as post-traumatic stress disorder, bipolar disorder, depression, etc.

Cathexis   A process in which an individual invests or spends his emotional or mental energy in an idea, object or another person is referred to as cathexis.

Classical Adlerian Psychology   The aim or objective is to help the clients overcome their insecurities by developing a deep connectedness. The psychotherapist indulges in a dialog with the client and corrects his mistaken attitudes, feelings and behavior regarding himself and the world.

Clinical Psychology   Scientific study of psychology and its application in order to understand, prevent and relieve dysfunction or distress that is psychologically-based is termed as clinical psychology.

Cognition   The processing of thoughts and in psychological terms it is referred to as processing of information.

Delirium   The loss of rational cognition and the capacity to perceive reality.

Delusion   A failure of the principle of reality such that any idea or image might be fixated upon as real whether it exists or not. A condition not uncommon in anxiety neurosis and schizophrenia.

Depression   A disassociated emotion of lethargy and a sense of meaninglessness the etiology of which is uncertain but exacerbated by anxiety and fear.

Developmental Psychology   A branch of psychology focusing upon the stages of maturation from infancy to old age.

Early Intervention in Psychosis   The recognition of the need for psychotherapeutic and/or medical oversight in extreme cases of psychotic behavior for the protection of the patient.

Egocentrism   A state of behavior in which the individual is overly concentrated on his/her own central importance to their social environment at the expense of caring for others.

F-scale   A commonly used personality test used to measure authoritarian personality traits.

Family Therapy   An modality of analysis and treatment within psychotherapy which focuses upon the family unit of parents and children rather than dealing with single individuals.
It is a kind of psychotherapy which helps in nurturing the change and development that takes place among family relationships. The interactions that take place between family members have an impact on their psychological health.

Folk Psychology   Home spun insights offered by older people in an attempt to help others with their emotional and often family problems based on common sense and personal experience.

Group Psychotherapy   The use of therapeutic technique of analysis within the context of several individuals who share and suffer from similar anxieties or neuroses.

Guilt   An emotion which elevates the realization that a moral code has been violated to the level of reflective consciousness often manifesting itself in feelings of anxiety.

Hierarchy of Needs   Abraham Maslow notion that human development occurs along an identified trajectory of needs and their fulfillment with each dependent upon the other in an identified sequence of development.

Humanistic Psychology   A school of psychology based on the confidence in the human personality's ability to discover and act upon factors positively affecting their well-being developed by Abraham Maslow and Carl Rogers.

Hysteria   An emotional display of anxiety wherein

the patient has little or no control over thoughts or behavior manifesting a neurosis.

Id   One of the three components of the psyche, i.e., id, ego, and super-ego, identified by Sigmund Freud in the development of psychoanalysis in which the instincts constitute the source of libidinal energy expressed irrationally and in need of supervision by the ego.

Kubler-Ross Model   Known as 'five stages of grief' was introduced by Elizabeth Kubler-Ross. The model is used to describe a process through which people deal with tragedy and grief in five discrete stages. The five stages of the process in their sequential form are, 'Denial', 'Anger', 'Bargaining', 'Depression' and 'Acceptance'.

Kohlberg's Stages of Moral Development   Stages of moral development which are based on a psychological theory which proposes that moral reasoning which is the basis of ethical behavior is developed in six stages. Each of the succeeding stage in the sequence is efficient or adequate than the earlier one in dealing with moral dilemmas faced by an individual.

Lacunar Lmnesia   The subject loses his memory about a certain specific event and which results into the creation of a gap or lacuna.

Lapsus Linguae   An error which occurs in the memory, speech or physical action because of an unconscious conflict, wish or train of thought that is interfering with their functioning.

Latent Learning   Knowledge that is not expressed

immediately in an overt manner. The things that are learned by an individual stay in the subconscious mind and might be expressed in response to specific experiences or events.

Lateral Thinking A creative or indirect approach towards problem solving, instead of going by the method of following a step-by-step logic.

Logotherapy One of the psychotherapies which focuses on finding the meaning in one's life rather than emphasizing on the doctrine of 'will to pleasure' or 'will to power'.

Mania A person suffers from the problem of elevated mood, unusual thought patterns and psychosis is termed as mania.

Masochism
It is the feeling of gratification experienced by an individual as a result of infliction of pain or humiliation upon himself.

Melancholia A mood disorder in which the patient suffers from low levels of eagerness and enthusiasm in performing activities of day-to-day life.

Mental Health Indicates a condition of emotional and cognitive well-being or the absence of any kind of mental disorder.

Mind The manifestation of the different aspects of consciousness and intellect in the form of various combinations of perception, thoughts, emotions, memory, imagination and will.

Narcissism   The attribute or trait of personality which is characterized with self-love and other such characteristics that are associated with ego or self-image.

Narrative Therapy   A type of psychotherapy in which the therapist engages himself in a process which involves the client and is aimed at discovering the richer or positive narratives which originate from disparate descriptions of various experiences.

Neo-Freudian
The psychologists who followed the basic principles posited by Sigmond Freud but changed or altered them to some extent.

Neuropsychology   The science which deals with overt behaviors and psychological processes related to the structure and functions of brain.

Nightmare   It is a dream that is unpleasant in nature and results into a strong emotional response that is mostly associated with fear or horror.

Noetic Psychology   Finding out the meaning and purpose, integration of cognition (thinking) with effect (emotion) and the resolution of existential angst.

Obsessive Compulsive Disorder   A mental disorder in which an individual suffers from anxiety that results from various intrusive thoughts.

Operant Conditioning   Used for modifying the form and occurrences of behavior by making use of the consequences.

Panic Attacks   The periods of intense anxiety, fear, physiological arousal, discomfort, stomach problems, etc. which occur suddenly and are discrete in nature.

Paranoia   A thought process which is characterized by excessive fear or anxiety.

Psychoanalysis   The Freudian system of the study of behavior and functioning of the human psychology by means of investigating the mind is termed as psychoanalysis. Psychoanalysis is carried out for systematizing the theories of human behavior and to treat the different psychological and emotional illnesses.

Psychoanalytic Theory   Concerned with the definition and dynamics of the development of personality. The psychoanalytic theory was developed by Sigmond Freud.

Psychodynamics   Psychological forces that underlie the human behavior are systematically studied in the branch of psychology. The emphasis is given on the interplay that happens between the conscious and unconscious motivation.

Psychodynamic Psychotherapy   Therapy used for alleviating psychic tension by revealing the unconscious content of a client's or patient's psyche.

Psycholinguistics   The study of different neurobiological and psychological factors that enable human beings in acquiring, using, comprehending and finally producing a language.

Psychology of Learning   The study of effects of conditioning, environment and reinforcement provides the psychologists with the best information about the human behavior.

Quantitative Psychology The study of techniques and ways to measure human attributes and mathematical and statistical patterning of psychological processes and analysis of psychological data.

Quantum Psychology An approach which involves being aware of our automatic responses and its triggers in addition to the inherent mechanism of those responses.

Regression A defense mechanism through which the ego temporarily reverts to an earlier state of development. During regression, the thoughts are pushed from consciousness to unconsciousness.

Retrograde Amnesia The affected person is unable to recall or retrieve the events which had occurred before the amnesia.

Sauce-Bearnaise Syndrome A conditioned taste aversion can occur when an individual associates the taste of a certain food item with the symptoms caused by a toxic, or spoiled substance.

Savant Syndrome A disorder wherein a particular person with diminished mental skill demonstrates extraordinary proficiency in one specific isolated skill.

Schizoid Personality Disorder A disorder characterized by extreme shyness, reclusive nature, discomfort with other people around and incapability of forming close relationships.

Schizophrenia   A Disorder characterized by problems with perceptions or expressions of reality, significant social problems, disorganized thinking, and delusions or hallucinations.

Schizotypal Personality Disorder   A disorder characterized by unconventional beliefs, odd behavior, thinking and a need for social isolation.

Seasonal Affective Disorder   Depression occurring during certain times of the year when there is less sunlight.

Selective Distortion   The tendency of the individuals to interpret a piece of information in a particular way which will support their existing beliefs.

Self-actualization   A holistic approach towards life, thus allowing oneself to reach the highest potential, without possessing any greed of success.

Self-loathing   A disorder characterized by extreme dislike of oneself.

Semantic Dyslexia   A subtype of dyslexia characterized by inability to properly attach words to their meanings when reading.

Semantic Memory   The memory of meanings, understandings, and other various concept-based knowledge is known as semantic memory or long-term memory.

Separation Anxiety Disorder   A psychological

condition wherein an individual experiences excessive anxiety regarding separation from home or from people with whom he is closely attached.

Sexual Response Cycle   A four-phase model of physiological responses (excitement phase, plateau phase, orgasmic phase, and resolution phase) triggered during sexual stimulation.

Short-term Memory   The capacity of the human mind to hold a small amount of information in an active, easily accessible state for a brief period of time is referred to as short-term memory.

Situation Awareness   The perception of environmental elements within a volume of time and space, comprehension of their meaning, and the projection of their status in the near future.

Social Anxiety   A psychiatric disorder characterized by persistent, intense, and chronic fear of being judged, embarrassed or humiliated by others, owing to one's own actions.

Social Cognition   Processing social information, emphasizing on encoding, storage, retrieval and application in social situations.

Social Inhibition   A process or behavior that is considered to be objectionable in the social settings is known as social inhibition.

Social Psychology   That branch of psychology that studies individuals and their relationships with each other, with groups and with the society as a whole.

Somatoform Disorder
Somatoform disorder is a psychiatric disorder characterized by physical symptoms that mimic disease or injury whose physical cause cannot be identified.

Somatotherapy   The treatment of mental illness by physical means, such as medication or psychosurgery, rather than psychotherapy is known as somatotherapy.

Spatial-temporal Reasoning   The ability of visualizing the spatial patterns and manipulating them mentally in a time-ordered sequence of spatial transformations.

Spontaneous Recovery   The reappearance of a conditioned response which had been previously extinguished owing to various factors, including injury.

SUDS   The Subjective Units of Disturbance Scale is a scale of 10 used to measure the subjective intensity of disturbance experienced by an individual.

Suicide   The act of killing oneself is termed as suicide or self-annihilation.

Superiority Complex   Subconscious neurotic mechanism of compensation developed by the individual owing to extensive feelings of inferiority is referred to as superiority complex.

Syndrome   Several clinically recognizable features, signs, symptoms, phenomena or characteristics that occurs together is referred to as syndrome.

Systematic Desensitization   A type of behavioral therapy which helps the subject to effectively overcome various phobias and anxiety disorders.

Systems Intelligence   The human action that connects sensitivity pertaining to systemic environment with systems thinking, thus enhancing a person's problem solving capabilities.

Tarantism   A nervous disorder, characterized by an intense urge to dance, which is most often attributed to bite of the tarantula species of spider..

Temperament   The inborn component of an individual's personality.

Tension Myositis   The patient exhibits psychosomatic musculoskeletal and nerve symptoms.

Theory of Cognitive Development   Piaget's idea that there are four different stages of mental representation which a child passes through on his way to an adult level of intelligence..

Theory of Multiple Intelligences   Defines the concept of intelligence and addresses whether methods which claim to measure intelligence are truly scientific or not.

Thought Withdrawal   The delusion which makes a person feel that thoughts have been 'taken out' of his mind is referred to as thought withdrawal.

Tolerance   The ability of a person to tolerate various beliefs or practices which are followed by fellow human beings.

Transference　　The process of passing emotions from one person to another.

Transference Neurosis　　Used by Sigmund Freud to describe a new form of the analysand's infantile neurosis that is observed during the psychoanalytic process.

Transvestism　　Adopting the clothes and the behavior of a person of opposite sex.

Trauma　　A term used to refer to emotional shock often characterized by long-lasting effects.

Unconditional Positive Regard　　A concept developed by Carl Rogers suggesting a broad acceptance and support of an individual irrespective of what the individual says or does.

Unconscious Mind　　A part of the mind that triggers a collection of thoughts which inhibit our mind without us being aware of them.

Undifferentiated Schizophrenia　　A condition wherein the patient does show psychotic symptoms, but without meeting the criteria for paranoid or catatonic types.

Universal Law of Generalization　　The probability of the response to one stimulus will be generalized to another.

Value　　An evaluative process which reveals more about nature, quality, abilities of a particular person than what is really known.

Value Theory　　A theory that states how people value various things and concepts, the reasons they utilize for this evaluation, and the scope of applications of various legitimate evaluations across the society.

Vegeto-therapy   A form of psychotherapy which involves the physical manifestations of various emotions.

Vertical thinking   A distinct approach towards problem solving using selective, analytical and sequential methods.

Visual Learning
Visual learning is a process of learning, wherein the ideas, concepts as well as the data are presented in the form of images and techniques.

Visual Thinking   The process of thinking by processing the information visually, instead of processing it linguistically or verbally.

Volition   One of the three primary human psychological faculties, which stresses on the study of will, choice and decision.

Voyeurism   An act of perversion which helps an individual to obtain sexual gratification by seeing the genital organs of others or watching them indulging in a sexual act.

WAIS   Wechsler Adult Intelligence Scale, abbreviated as WAIS, is a general intelligence test which was first released in 1955 as a revision of the Wechsler-Bellevue test that was released in 1939.

Wechsler Intelligence Scale for Children   A general intelligence test, that can be completed without reading or writing, designed for children in the age groups of 6 to 16.

Wechsler Preschool and Primary Scale of Intelligence

An intelligence test developed by David Wechsler in the year 1967. It is used to test children between the age group 2 years, 6 months and 7 years, 3 months.

Wernicke's Aphasia   The inability to communicate verbally owing to impairment of receptive abilities.

Womb Envy   In psychology, the term womb envy is used to refer to the alleged unconscious, unexpressed desire of a man to possess a womb.

Word Salad   Word salad, also known as schizophasia, refers the utterance of a jumble of meaningless words and phrases by an individual.

Working Memory   Working memory is the ability of an individual to hold a small amount of material in memory for a short period of time, while he simultaneously processes the same or any other material.

Yerkes-Dodson Law   The Yerkes-Dodson law is a relationship between arousal and performance which was derived from experiment and observation by psychologists, Robert M. Yerkes and John Dillingham Dodson.

Zero-defects Mentality   Zero-defects mentality is a state which is when a command-and-control structure stops tolerating mistakes.

COMPREHENSIVE REFERENCE BIBLIOGRAPHY

Abel, Kathryn M. (2010). "Birth weight, schizophrenia, and adult mental disorder: is risk confined to the smallest babies?". *Archives of General Psychiatry. 67 (9): 923–930.*

Adams, Henry E., Sutker, Patricia B. (2001). *Comprehensive Handbook of Psychopathology. Third Edition.* Springer.

Adler, David A., ed. (1990). *Treating Personality Disorders.* San Francisco: Jossey-Bass.

Akhtar, Salman (1987). "Schizoid Personality Disorder: A Synthesis of Developmental, Dynamic, and Descriptive Features." *American Journal of Psychotherapy. 41: 499–518.*

Akhtar, S. (1990). "Paranoid Personality Disorder: A Synthesis of Developmental, Dynamic, and Descriptive Features." *American Journal of Psychotherapy*, 44, 5-25.

Akiskal HS, Yerevanian BI, Davis GC, King D, Lemmi H (February 1985). "The nosologic status of borderline personality: clinical and polysomnographic study." *Am J Psychiatry. 142 (2): 192–8.*

Alam C.M.; Merskey H. (1992). "The development of hysterical personality." *History of Psychiatry. 3: 135–165.*

Alarcón RD, Sarabia S (2012). "Debates on the narcissism conundrum: trait, domain, dimension, type, or disorder?." *J Nerv Ment Dis (200): 16–25.*

Allday, Erin (November 26, 2011). "Revision of psychiatric manual under fire". *San Francisco Chronicle.*

Allen DM, Farmer RG (1996). "Family relationships of adults with borderline personality disorder." *Compr Psychiatry. 37 (1): 43–51.*

Alexander, Brian (May 22, 2008). "What's 'normal' sex? Shrinks seek definition: Controversy erupts over creation of psychiatric rule book's new edition". *MSNBC. Retrieved June 14, 2008.*

Alterman, AI; Rutherford, MJ; Cacciola, JS; McKay, JR; Boardman, CR (1998). "Prediction of 7 months methadone maintenance treatment response by four measures of antisociality." *Drug and Alcohol Dependence. 49 (3): 217–23.*

Aluja, Anton; Garcia, Luis F.; Blanch, Angel; De Lorenzo, D.; Fibla, Joan (1 July 2009). "Impulsive-disinhibited personality and serotonin transporter gene polymorphisms: association study in an inmate's sample." *Journal of Psychiatric Research. 43 (10): 906–914.*

Amad, A; Ramoz, N; Thomas, P; Jardri, R; Gorwood, P (March 2014). "Genetics of borderline personality disorder: systematic review and proposal of an integrative model." *Neuroscience and biobehavioral reviews. 40: 6–19.*

Amann-Gainotti, M.; Ducret, J.-J. (1992). "Jean Piaget, disciple of Pierre Janet: Influence of behavior psychology and relations with psychoanalysis". *Information Psychiatrique. 68: 598–606.*

American Psychiatric Association Practice Guidelines (October 2001). "Practice guideline for the treatment of patients with borderline personality disorder. American Psychiatric Association." *Am J Psychiatry. 158 (10 Suppl): 1–52.*

Anderluh MB, et al. (2003). "Childhood obsessive–compulsive personality traits in adult women with eating disorders: defining a broader eating disorder phenotype." *Am J Psychiatry. 160 (2): 242–47.*

Anglina, Deidre M., Patricia R. Cohenab, and Henian Chena (2008). "Duration of early maternal separation and prediction of schizotypal symptoms from early adolescence to midlife." *Schizophrenia Research,* Volume 103, Issue 1, Pages 143-150.

Aoki, Yuta; Inokuchi, Ryota; Nakao, Tomohiro; Yamasue, Hidenori (25 February 2017). "Neural bases of antisocial behavior: a voxel-based meta-analysis." *Social Cognitive and Affective Neuroscience. 9 (8): 1223–1231.*

Aragona M. (2014) "Epistemological reflections about the crisis of the DSM-5 and the revolutionary potential of the RDoC project Dialogues."*Philosophy, Mental and Neuro Sciences* 7: 11-20

Arnett, Jeffrey Jensen (2000). "Emerging Adulthood: A Theory of Development from the Late Teens Through the Twenties". *American Psychologist. 55 (5): 469–480.*

Arntz, Arnoud (September 2005). "Introduction to special issue: cognition and emotion in borderline personality disorder." *Journal of Behavior Therapy and Experimental Psychiatry. 36 (3): 167–72.*

Aronson TA (August 1985). "Historical perspectives on the borderline concept: a review and critique." *Psychiatry. 48 (3): 209–22.*

Atwell Irene; Azibo Daudi A (1991). "Diagnosing personality disorder in Africans (Blacks) using the Azibo nosology: Two case studies". *Journal of Black Psychology.* 17 (2): 1–22.

Aviram, RB; Brodsky, BS; Stanley, B (2006). "Borderline personality disorder, stigma, and treatment implications." *Harvard Review of Psychiatry. 14 (5): 249–56.*

Ayduk O, Zayas V, Downey G, Cole AB, Shoda Y, Mischel W (February 2008). "Rejection Sensitivity and Executive Control: Joint predictors of Borderline Personality features." *J Res Pers. 42 (1): 151–168.*

Azibo, Daudi Ajani ya (November 2014). "The Azibo Nosology II: Epexegesis and 25th Anniversary Update: 55 Culture-focused Mental Disorders Suffered by African Descent People" (PDF). *Journal of Pan African Studies.* 7 (5): 32–176.

Baca-Garcia, E.; Perez-Rodriguez, M. M.; Basurte-Villamor, I.; Del Moral, A. L. F.; Jimenez-Arriero, M. A.; De Rivera, J. L. G.; Saiz-Ruiz, J.; Oquendo, M. A. (March 2007). "Diagnostic stability of psychiatric disorders in clinical practice". *The British Journal of Psychiatry.* 190 (3): 210–6.

Baer, Lee. (1998). "Personality Disorders in Obsessive–Compulsive Disorder." *In Obsessive–Compulsive Disorders: Practical Management. Third edition.* Jenike, Michael et al. (eds.). St. Lou is: Mosby.

Baker, Laura A.; Bezdjian, Serena; Raine, Adrian (1 January 2006). "Behavioral Genetics: The Science of Antisocial Behavior." *Law and Contemporary Problems. 69 (1–2): 7–46.*

Bakkevig J.F.; Sigmund K. (2010). "Is the diagnostic and statistical manual of mental disorders, fourth edition, histrionic personality disorder category a valid construct?." *Comprehensive Psychiatry. 51: 462–470.*

Ball JS, Links PS (February 2009). "Borderline personality disorder and childhood trauma: evidence for a causal relationship." *Curr Psychiatry Rep. 11 (1): 63–8.*

Barlow, H.D. & Durand, V.M. (2005). "Personality Disorders." *Abnormal Psychology: An Integrative Approach (4th ed.).* Belmont, CA: Thomas Wadsworth.

Battle, Cynthia L.; Shea, M. Tracie; Johnson, Dawn M.; Yen, Shirley; Zlotnick, Caron; Zanarini, Mary C.; Sanislow, Charles A.; Skodol, Andrew E.; et al. (2004). "Childhood Maltreatment Associated With Adult Personality Disorders: Findings From the Collaborative Longitudinal Personality Disorders Study." *Journal of Personality Disorders. 18 (2): 193–211.*

Bayer, Ronald (1981). *Homosexuality and American Psychiatry: The Politics of Diagnosis.* Princeton University Press p. 105.

Beck, Aaron T; Freeman, Arthur (1990). *Cognitive Therapy of Personality Disorders.* New York: Guilford Press.

Becker D (October 2000). "When she was bad: borderline personality disorder in a posttraumatic age." *Am J Orthopsychiatry. 70 (4): 422–32.*

Beilin, H. (1992). "Piaget's enduring contribution to developmental psychology". *Developmental Psychology. 28 (2): 191–204.*

Beilin, H. (1994). Jean Piaget's enduring contribution to developmental psychology. A century of developmental psychology. Washington, DC US: American Psychological Association.

Benazzi F (January 2006). "Borderline personality-bipolar spectrum relationship." *Prog. Neuropsychopharmacol. Biol. Psychiatry. 30 (1): 68–74.*

Bender, Donna S.; Skodol, Andrew E.; Dyck, Ingrid R.; Markowitz, John C.; Shea, M. Tracie; Yen, Shirley; Sanislow, Charles A.; Pinto, Anthony; Zanarini, Mary C.; McGlashan, Thomas H.; Gunderson, John G.; Daversa, Maria T.; Grilo, Carlos M. (2007). "Ethnicity and Mental Health Treatment Utilization by Patients with Personality Disorders." *Journal of Consulting and Clinical Psychology. 75 (6): 992–999.*

Bender, D; Dolan R; Skodol A (2001). "Treatment utilization by patients with personality disorders." *Am J Psychiatry. 158. 158 (Am J Psychiatry 2001): 295–302.*

Bender, D.; Skodol, A. E.; Pagano, M. E.; Dyck, I. R.; Grilo, C. M.; Shea, M. T.; Sanislow, C. A.; Zanarini, M. C.; Yen, S.; McGlashan, T. H.; Gunderson, J. G. (2006). "Prospective assessment of treatment use by patients with personality disorders." *Psychiatr Serv. 57. 2 (Psychiatr Serv): 254–257.*

Benjamin, Lorna Smith (1993). *Interpersonal Diagnosis and Treatment of Personality Disorders.* Guilford Press.

Benjamin, Lorna Smith (1996). "Dependent Personality Disorder." *Interpersonal Diagnosis and Treatment of Personality Disorders.* Guilford Press. pp. 221–39.

Benjamin, Lorna Smith (1996). "Dependent Personality Disorder." *Interpersonal Diagnosis and Treatment of Personality Disorders.* Guilford Press. *pp. 221–39.*

Bentall, R. (2006). "Madness explained : Why we must reject the Kraepelinian paradigm and replace it with a 'complaint-orientated' approach to understanding mental illness". *Medical Hypotheses.* 66 (2): 220–233.

Berenbaum, Howard, Eve M. Valera and John G. Kerns (2003). "Psychological Trauma and Schizotypal Symptoms," *Schizophrenia Bulletin,* Volume 29, Number 1 Pp. 143-152.

Bernstein, David P.; Arntz, Arnoud; Vos, Marije de (2007). "Schema Focused Therapy in Forensic Settings: Theoretical Model and Recommendations for Best Clinical Practice." *International Journal of Forensic Mental Health. 6 (2): 169–183.*

Berger, Fred K. (29 July 2016). "Antisocial personality disorder: MedlinePlus Medical Encyclopedia." *MedlinePlus.*

Bernstein, D. P., Useda, D., Siever, L. J. (1995). "Paranoid Personality Disorder." In: J. W. Livesley (Ed.). *The DSM-IV Personality Disorders.* (pp. 45-57). New York: Guilford.

Bhugra, D. & Munro, A. (1997). Troublesome Disguises: Underdiagnosed Psychiatric Syndromes. *Blackwell Science Ltd.*

Binks CA, Fenton M, McCarthy L, Lee T, Adams CE, Duggan C (2006). Binks C, ed. "Pharmacological interventions for people with borderline personality disorder." *Cochrane Database of Systematic Reviews (1):* CD005653.

Black DW, Gunter T, Allen J, et al. (2007). "Borderline personality disorder in male and female offenders newly committed to prison." *Compr Psychiatry. 48 (5): 400–5.*

Blais M.A.; Hilsenroth M.; Fowler C. (1998). "Rorschach correlates of the DSM-IV histrionic personality disorder." *Journal of Personality Assessment. 70 (2): 355–365.*

Blaney, Paul H. (2014). *Oxford Textbook of Psychopathology.* Oxford University Press.

Blechner, Mark J. (July 1994). "Projective identification, countertransference, and the 'maybe-me'." *Contemporary Psychoanalysis. 30 (3): 619–30.*

Bleuler, Eugen (1924). *Textbook of Psychiatry*, New York: Macmillan.

Bloland, Sue Erikson (2005). *In the Shadow of Fame: A Memoir by the Daughter of Erik H. Erikson.* New York: Viking Press.

Blom, Jan Dirk (2010). *A Dictionary of Hallucinations (1 ed.).* New York: Springer.

Bolton S, Gunderson JG (September 1996). "Distinguishing borderline personality disorder from bipolar disorder:

differential diagnosis and implications." *Am J Psychiatry.*
153 (9): 1202–7.

Bornstein, Robert F. (1996-01-01). "Sex Differences in
Dependent Personality Disorder Prevalence Rates." *Clinical
Psychology: Science and Practice. 3 (1).*

"Borderline Personality Disorder". NIMH, 16 March 2016.

"BPD Awareness Month – Congressional History". (2010).
*BPD Today. Mental Health Today. Retrieved 1 November
2010.*

Bradley R, Jenei J, Westen D (January 2005). "Etiology of
borderline personality disorder: disentangling the
contributions of intercorrelated antedents." *J. Nerv. Ment.
Dis. 193 (1): 24–31.*

Brenman-Gibson, Margaret (1997). "The Legacy of Erik
Hamburger Erikson". *Psychoanalytic Review. 84 (3): 329–
335.*

Bringuier, J.-C. (1980). *Conversations with Jean Piaget.*
Chicago: University of Chicago Press.

Breedlove, S. Marc (2015). *Principles of Psychology.* Oxford
University Press.

Brown MZ, Comtois KA, Linehan MM (February 2002).
"Reasons for suicide attempts and nonsuicidal self-injury in
women with borderline personality disorder." *J Abnorm
Psychol. 111 (1): 198–202.*

Brown, Serena-Lynn; Botsis, Alexander; Van Praag; Herman M. (1994). "Serotonin and Aggression." *Journal of Offender Rehabilitation. 3–4. 21 (3): 27–39.*

Burston, Daniel (2007). *Erik Erikson and the American Psyche: Ego, Ethics, and Evolution.* Lanham, Maryland: Jason Aronson.

Cain, Nicole; Ansell, Emily B.; Simpson, H. Blair; Pinto, Anthony (2014). "Interpersonal Functioning in Obsessive–Compulsive Personality Disorder." *Journal of Personality Assessment. 97 (1): 1–10.*

Caligor, E; Levy, KN; Yeomans, FE (May 2015). "Narcissistic personality disorder: diagnostic and clinical challenges." *The American Journal of Psychiatry. 172 (5): 415–22.*

Callaghan G. M.; Summers C. J.; Weidman M. (2003). "The treatment of histrionic and narcissistic personality disorder behaviors: A single-subject demonstration of clinical improvement using functional analytic psychotherapy." *Journal of contemporary psychotherapy. 33 (4): 321–339.*

Calvo, Rosa; Lázaro, Luisa; Castro-Fornieles, Josefina; Fonta, Elena; Moreno, Elena; Toro, J. (April 2009). "Obsessive-compulsive personality disorder traits and personality dimensions in parents of children with obsessive-compulsive disorder." *European Psychiatry. 24 (3): 201–206.*

Carey, Benedict (December 17, 2008). "Psychiatrists Revise the Book of Human Troubles". *The New York Times.*

Carey, Benedict (May 8, 2012), "Psychiatry Manual Drafters Back Down on Diagnoses", *The New York Times, nytimes.com, retrieved May 12, 2012*

Carlson, Neil R.; Heth, C. Donald (2010). *Psychology: The Science of Behavior.* Pearson Canada.

Cassels, Caroline (2 December 2012). "DSM-5 Gets APA's Official Stamp of Approval". *Medscape.* WebMD, LLC. Retrieved 2012-12-05.

Caspi A, McClay J, Moffitt TE, Mill J, Martin J, Craig IW, et al. (Aug 2002). "Role of genotype in the cycle of violence in maltreated children." *Science. 297 (5582): 851–4.*

Chafos VH, Economou P (July 2014). "Beyond Borderline Personality Disorder: The Mindful Brain." *Social Work. 59 (4): 297–302.*

Chanen, Andrew M; Thompson, Katherine N (1 April 2016). "Prescribing and borderline personality disorder." *Australian Prescriber. 39 (2): 49–53.*

Chapman, M. (1988). *Constructive evolution: Origins and development of Piaget's thought.* Cambridge: Cambridge University Press.

Chen, C. K., Lin, S. K., Sham, P. C.; et al. (2005). "Morbid risk for psychiatric disorder among the relatives of methamphetamine users with and without psychosis." *American Journal of Medical Genetics. 136: 87–91.*

Lou Chibbaro, Jr. (May 30, 2008). "Activists alarmed over APA: Head of psychiatry panel favors 'change' therapy for some trans teens". *Washington Blade.*

Chodoff, P. (2005) "Psychiatric Diagnosis: A 60-Year Perspective," *Psychiatric News* June 3, 2005 Volume 40 Number 11, p17

Cleary M, Siegfried N, Walter G (September 2002). "Experience, knowledge and attitudes of mental health staff regarding clients with a borderline personality disorder." *Int J Ment Health Nurs. 11 (3): 186–91.*

Cohen P (September 2008). "Child development and personality disorder." *Psychiatr Clin North Am. 31 (3): 477–93.*

Coles, Robert (1970). *Erik H. Erikson: The Growth of His Work.* Boston: Little, Brown and Company.

Coles, Robert; Fitzpatrick, J. J. (1976). "The Writings of Erik H. Erikson". *The Psychohistory Review. 5 (3): 42–46.*

Comer, Ronald (2014). *Fundamentals of abnormal psychology (PDF).* New York, NY: Worth Publishers.

Compton, Michael T. (2007) Recovery: Patients, Families, Communities Conference Report, *Medscape Psychiatry & Mental Health*, October 11–14, 2007.

Connors, Mary E. (1997). "The Renunciation of Love: Dismissive Attachment and its Treatment." *Psychoanalytic Psychology. 14: 475–493.*

Connolly, Adrian J. (2008). "Personality disorders in homeless drop-in center clients." *Journal of Personality Disorders. 22 (6): 573–588.*

Coolidge, Frederick L. (2012). "Are alexithymia and schizoid personality disorder synonymous diagnoses?" *Comprehensive Psychiatry. 54 (2): 141–148.*

Cooper, JE; Kendell, RE; Gurland, BJ; Sartorius, N; Farkas, T (April 1969). "Cross-national study of diagnosis of the mental disorders: some results from the first comparative investigation". *The American Journal of Psychiatry.* 10 Suppl: 21–9.

Corbitt, E., Widiger, T. (1995). "Sex differences among the personality disorders: An exploration of the data." *Clinical Psychology: Science and Practice. 2 (3): 225–238.*

Cordier, Thomas A. (2016). "The Creation and Implementation of the Interpersonal-Cognitive-Behavioral Treatment System (I-CBT)," in *Foundation Theology 2016,* edited by John H. Morgan. South Bend, IN: GTF Books.

Cosgrove, Lisa; Krimsky, Sheldon; Vijayaraghavan, Manisha; Schneider, Lisa (April 2006), "Financial Ties between DSM-IV Panel Members and the Pharmaceutical Industry", *Psychotherapy and Psychosomatics,* 75 (3): 154–160.

Cosgrove, Lisa; Drimsky Lisa (March 2012). "A comparison of DSM-iv and DSM-5 panel members' financial associations with industry: A pernicous problem persisits". *PLoS Medicine.* 9 (3): 1–5.

Cosmides, Leda; John Tooby (1999). "Toward an Evolutionary Taxonomy of Treatable Conditions" (PDF). *Journal of Abnormal Psychology.* 108 (3): 453–464.

Crimlisk H.; Ron M. (1999). "Conversion hysteria: history, diagnostic issues, and clinical practice." *Cognitive Neuropsychiatry. 4 (3): 165–180.*

Dalal PK, Sivakumar T (2009). "Moving towards ICD-11 and DSM-5: Concept and evolution of psychiatric classification". *Indian Journal of Psychiatry. 51 (4): 310–319.*

Daley SE, Burge D, Hammen C (August 2000). "Borderline personality disorder symptoms as predictors of 4-year romantic relationship dysfunction in young women: addressing issues of specificity." *J Abnorm Psychol. 109 (3): 451–60. PMID 11016115.*

Diagnostic and Statistical Manual of Mental Disorders (DSM-5), (New York: Americal Psychiatric Association, 2013, 5th edition).

Darke, S; Finlay-Jones, R; Kaye, S; Blatt, T (1996). "Anti-social personality disorder and response to methadone maintenance treatment." *Drug and alcohol review. 15 (3): 271–6.*

Deans C, Meocevic E (2006). "Attitudes of registered psychiatric nurses towards patients diagnosed with borderline personality disorder." *Contemp Nurse. 21 (1): 43–9.*

Demazeux, Steeves and Singy, Patrick (2015). *Perspective: Philosophical Reflections on the Psychiatric Babel.* Springer.

De Reus, Rob J.M.; Paul M.G. Emmelkamp (February 2012). "Obsessive–compulsive personality disorder: A review of current empirical findings." *Personality and Mental Health. 6 (1): 1–21.*

Derefinko, Karen J.; Thomas A. Widiger (2008). "Antisocial Personality Disorder." *The Medical Basis of Psychiatry: 213–226.*

DeSoto, M. Catherine (2007). "Borderline Personality Disorder, Gender and Serotonin: Does Estrogen Play a Role?." *In Czerbska, Martina T. Psychoneuroendocrinology Research Trends. Nova Biomedical.* Nova Science Publishers. pp. 149–60.

DeSoto MC, Geary DC, Hoard MK, Sheldon MS, Cooper L (August 2003). "Estrogen fluctuations, oral contraceptives and borderline personality." *Psychoneuroendocrinology. 28 (6): 751–66.*

Dhawan N, Kunik ME, Oldham J, Coverdale J (2010), "Prevalence and Treatment of Narcissistic Personality Disorder in the Community: A Systematic Review." *Comprehensive Psychiatry, 51 (4): 333–339.*

Diagnostic and Statistical Manual-5. Arlington, VA: American Psychiatric Association.
Millon, Théodore and Grossman, Seth (2004). Personality Disorders in Modern Life. Wiley.

Disney, K.L., Weinstein, Y., & Oltmanns, T.F. (2012). "Personality disorder symptoms are differentially related to divorce frequency." *Journal of Family Psychology. 26: 959–965.*

Domino, George (2002). "Creativity and Ego Defense Mechanisms: Some Exploratory Empirical Evidence." *Creativity Research Journal. 14 (1): 17–25.*

Douvan, Elizabeth (1997). "Erik Erikson: Critical Times, Critical Theory". *Child Psychiatry and Human Development. 28 (1): 15–21.*

Dozier, Mary; Stovall-McClough, K. Chase; Albus, Kathleen E. (1999*).* "Attachment and psychopathology in adulthood". *In Cassidy, Jude; Shaver, Phillip R. Handbook of attachment.* New York: Guilford Press. pp. 497–519.

DSM-5 Overview: The Future Manual | APA DSM-5 Archived December 17, 2009, at the *Wayback Machine.*

DSM-5 Ignores Biology of Mental Illness (2013). "The latest edition of psychiatry's standard guidebook neglects the biology of mental illness. New research may change that." May 5, 2013 *Scientific American.*

Ducasse, Déborah; Courtet, Philippe; Olié, Emilie (2014). "Physical and Social Pains in Borderline Disorder and Neuroanatomical Correlates: A Systematic Review." *Current Psychiatry Reports. 16 (5): 443.*

Eagle, Morris (1997). "Contributions of Erik Erikson". *Psychoanalytic Review. 84 (3): 337–347.*

Eggum, Natalie D.; Eisenberg, Nancy; Spinrad, Tracy L.; Valiente, Carlos; Edwards, Alison; Kupfer, Anne S.; Reiser, Mark (2009). "Predictors of withdrawal: Possible precursors of avoidant personality disorder." *Development and Psychopathology. 21 (3): 815–38.*

Ehret, Anna M.; Berking, Matthias (2013). Translated by Welsh, Susan. "From DSM-IV to DSM-5: What Has Changed in the New Edition?." *Verhaltenstherapie. Karger.* 23 (4): 258–266.

Ekleberry, Sharon (2014). "Dependent Personality Disorder (DPD)." *Treating Co-Occurring Disorders. pp. 63–4.*

Ekleberry, Sharon C. (2008). "Cluster A - Schizoid Personality Disorder and Substance Use Disorders." in *Integrated Treatment for Co-Occurring Disorders: Personality Disorders and Addiction.* Routledge.

Ellison, J. M.; Adler, D. A. (1990). "A strategy for the pharmacotherapy of personality disorders." In *Adler, David A. Treating Personality Disorders. San Francisco: Jossey-Bass. pp. 43–63.*

Erikson, Erik H. (1950). *Childhood and Society.* New York: W. W. Norton & Company.

Erikson, Erik H. (1958). *Young Man Luther: A Study in Psychoanalysis and History.* New York: W. W. Norton & Company.

Erikson, Erik H. (1966). *Insight and Responsibility.* New York: W. W. Norton & Company.

Erikson, Erik H. (1968). *Identity: Youth and Crisis.* New York: W. W. Norton & Company.

Erikson, Erik H. (1969). *Gandhi's Truth: On the Origins of Militant Nonviolence.* New York: W. W. Norton & Company.

Erikson, Erik H. (1975). *Life History and the Historical Moment.* New York: W. W. Norton & Company.

Erikson, Erik H. (1978). *Adulthood* (edited book). New York: W. W. Norton & Company.

Erikson, Erik H. with J. M. Erikson and H. Kivnick (1986). *Vital Involvement in Old Age.* New York: W. W. Norton & Company.

Erikson, Erik H. with J. M. Erikson (1987). *The Life Cycle Completed.* New York: W. W. Norton & Co.

Erikson, Erik H. (1974). *Dimensions of a New Identity. Jefferson Lectures in the Humanities.* New York: W. W. Norton & Company.

Erikson, Erik H.; Erikson, Joan M. (1997). *The Life Cycle Completed (extended ed.). New York:* W. W. Norton & Company.

Esterberg, Michelle L. (2010). "Cluster A Personality Disorders: Schizotypal, Schizoid and Paranoid Personality Disorders in Childhood and Adolescence." *Journal of Psychopathology and Behavioral Assessment 32 (4): 515–528.*

Fallon P (August 2003). "Travelling through the system: the lived experience of people with borderline personality disorder in contact with psychiatric services." *J Psychiatr Ment Health Nurs. 10 (4): 393–401.*

Fancher, R.E. & Rutherford, A. (2012). *Pioneers of Psychology.* New York, NY: W. W. Norton & Company.

Farrington, David P. and Coid, Jeremy (2004). *Early Prevention of Adult Antisocial Behavior*. Cambridge University Press. p. 82.

Fazel, Seena; Danesh, John (2002). "Serious mental disorder in 23 000 prisoners: A systematic review of 62 surveys." *The Lancet. 359 (9306): 545–550.*

Feldman, Ruth Duskin; Papalia, Diane E. (2010). *A child's world: infancy through adolescence (12th ed.).* New York: McGraw-Hill.

Ferrer M, Andión O, Matalí J, et al. (December 2010). "Comorbid attention-deficit/hyperactivity disorder in borderline patients defines an impulsive subtype of borderline personality disorder." *J. Pers. Disord. 24 (6): 812–22.*

Ficks CA, Waldman ID (Sep 2014). "Candidate genes for aggression and antisocial behavior: a meta-analysis of association studies of the 5HTTLPR and MAOA-uVNTR". *Behavioral Genetics. 44 (5): 427–44.*

Fineberg, N. A., Sharma, P., Sivakumaran, T., Sahakian, B., & Chamberlain, S. (2007). "Does Obsessive-Compulsive Personality Disorder Belong Within the Obsessive-Compulsive Spectrum." *CNS Spectrum. 12 (6): 467–474, 477–482.*

Fitzgerald, Michael; Aiden Corvin (2001-07-01). "Diagnosis and differential diagnosis of Asperger syndrome." *Advances in Psychiatric Treatment. 7 (4): 310–318.*

Flavell, J. (1967). *The Developmental Psychology of Jean Piaget*. New York: D. Van Nostrand Company.

Foa, EB; Kozak MJ; Goodman WK; Hollander E; Jenike MA; Rasmussen SA (1995). "obsessive-compulsive disorder." *DSM-IV field trial. 152 (Am J Psychiatry): 90–96.*

Fogelson, David L. ; Keith Nuechterlein (2007). "Avoidant personality disorder is a separable schizophrenia-spectrum personality disorder even when controlling for the presence of paranoid and schizotypal personality disorders." *Schizophrenia Research. 91: 192–199.*

Frances, Allen (17 May 2013). "The New Crisis in Confidence in Psychiatric Diagnosis". *Annals of Internal Medicine.*

Frances, Allen (11 May 2012). "Diagnosing the D.S.M.". *New York Times* (New York ed.). p. A19.

Frances, Allen (June 26, 2009). "A Warning Sign on the Road to DSM-V: Beware of Its Unintended Consequences". *Psychiatric Times.* Retrieved September 6, 2009.

Frances, Allen; Mack, Avram H.; Ross, Ruth; First, Michael B. (2000) [1995]. "The DSM-IV Classification and Psychopharmacology". In Bloom, Floyd E.; Kupfer, David J. *Psychopharmacology: The Fourth Generation of Progress.* American College of Neuropsychopharmacology.

Frances, Allen J. (December 2, 2012). "DSM 5 Is Guide Not Bible—Ignore Its Ten Worst Changes: APA approval of DSM-5 is a sad day for psychiatry". *Psychology Today.* Retrieved 2013-03-09.

Freedman, Robert; Lewis, David A.; Michels, Robert; Pine, Daniel S.; Schultz, Susan K.; Tamminga, Carol A.; Gabbard,

Glen O.; Gau, Susan Shur-Fen; Javitt, Daniel C.; Oquendo, Maria A.; Shrout, Patrick E.; Vieta, Eduard; Yager, Joel (January 2013). "The Initial Field Trials of DSM-5: New Blooms and Old Thorns". *American Journal of Psychiatry.* 170 (1): 1–5.

Friedheim, Donald K., Editor (1992). *History of Psychotheraphy: A Century of Change* (Washington, DC: American Psychological Association).

Friedman, Lawrence Jacob (2000). *Identity's Architect: A Biography of Erik H. Erikson.* Cambridge, Massachusetts: Harvard University Press.

Freud, S. (1959, original work published 1908).*Character and Anal Eroticism*, in The Standard Edition of the Complete Psychological Works of Sigmund Freud, 9, 170–71. James Strachey, ed. London: Hogarth.

Frazzetto G, Di Lorenzo G, Carola V, Proietti L, Sokolowska E, Siracusano A, et al. (2007). "Early trauma and increased risk for physical aggression during adulthood: the moderating role of MAOA genotype." *PLOS ONE. 2 (5): e486.*

Gabbard, Glen O., Gunderson John G. (2000). *Psychotherapy for Personality Disorders. First Edition.* American Psychiatric Publishing.

Gabbard, G.O. (2014). *Psychodynamic psychiatry in clinical practice. 5th Edition.* American Psychiatric Publishing: Washington, D.C.

Galarza M, Merlo A, Ingratta A, Albanese E, Albanese A (2004). "Cavum septum pellucidum and its increased prevalence in schizophrenia: a neuroembryological classification." *The Journal of neuropsychiatry and clinical neurosciences. 16 (1): 41–6.*

Gattico, E. (2001). *Jean Piaget*. Milano: Bruno Mondadori.

Ghaemi, S. Nassir; Knoll, James L., IV; Pearlman, Theodore (14 October 2013). "Why DSM-III, IV, and 5 are Unscientific". *Psychiatric Times*: Couch in Crisis Blog.

Gillberg, C.; Billstedt, E. (November 2000). "Autism and Asperger syndrome: coexistence with other clinical disorders." *Acta Psychiatrica Scandinavica. 102 (5): 321–330.*

Gjerde, L. C.; Czajkowski, N.; Røysamb, E.; Ørstavik, R. E.; Knudsen, G. P.; Østby, K.; Torgersen, S.; Myers, J.; Kendler, K. S.; Reichborn-Kjennerud, T. (2012). "The heritability of avoidant and dependent personality disorder assessed by personal interview and questionnaire." *Acta Psychiatrica Scandinavica. 126 (6): 448–57.*

Grijalva E, Newman DA, Tay L (2015), "Gender differences in narcissism: A meta-analytic review." *Psychological Bulletin, 141 (2): 261.*

Glenn, Andrea L. (January 2011). "The other allele: Exploring the long allele of the serotonin transporter gene as a potential risk factor for psychopathy: A review of the parallels in findings." *Neuroscience & Biobehavioral Reviews. 35: 612–620.*

Goethals, George W. (1976). "The Evolution of Sexual and Genital Intimacy: A Comparison of the Views of Erik H. Erikson and Harry Stack Sullivan". *The Journal of the American Academy of Psychoanalysis. 4 (4): 529–544.*

Goldberg, Susan; Muir, Roy; Kerr, John (2015). *Attachment Theory: Social, Developmental, and Clinical Perspectives.* Routledge.

Golomb, Elan (1992). *Trapped in the Mirror,* New York: Morrow.

Gooding DC; Tallent KA; Matts CW (2005). "Clinical status of at-risk individuals 5 years later: Further validation of the psychometric high-risk strategy." *Journal of Abnormal Psychology.* 114: 170–175.

Goodman, M; New, A; Siever, L (December 2004). "Trauma, genes, and the neurobiology of personality disorders." *Annals of the New York Academy of Sciences.* 1032: 104–16. *Bibcode:2004NYASA1032..104G.*

Grady-Weliky, TA (January 2003). "Premenstrual dysphoric disorder." *N. Engl. J. Med. 348 (5): 433–8.*

Grant BF, Chou SP, Goldstein RB, et al. (April 2008). "Prevalence, correlates, disability, and comorbidity of DSM-IV borderline personality disorder: results from the Wave 2 National Epidemiologic Survey on Alcohol and Related Conditions."*J Clin Psychiatry. 69 (4): 533–45.*

Grant, Bridget F.; Hasin, Deborah S.; Stinson, Frederick S.; Dawson, Deborah A.; Chou, S. Patricia; Ruan, W. June; Pickering, Roger P. (2004). "Prevalence, Correlates, and Disability of Personality Disorders in the United States." *The Journal of Clinical Psychiatry. 65 (7): 948–58.*

Grob, GN. (1991) "Origins of DSM-I: a study in appearance and reality," *Am J Psychiatry.* April;148(4):421–31.

Grossman R, Yehuda R, Siever L (June 1997). "The dexamethasone suppression test and glucocorticoid receptors in borderline personality disorder." *Annals of the New York Academy of Sciences. 821: 459–64.*

Grant, Chou, Goldstein, Huang, Stinson, Saha, Smith, Dawson, Pulay, Pickering, Ruan (April 2008). "Prevalence, correlates, disability, and comorbidity of DSM-IV borderline personality disorder: Results from the Wave 2 National Epidemiologic survey on alcohol and related conditions." *Journal of Clinical Psychology (69): 533–545.*

Greenberg, S; Shuman, DW; Meyer, RG (2004). "Unmasking forensic diagnosis". International *Journal of Law and Psychiatry.* 27 (1): 1–15.

Greenberg, Gary (January 29, 2012). "The D.S.M.'s Troubled Revision". *The New York Times.*

Grilo CM. (2004). "Diagnostic efficiency of DSM-IV criteria for obsessive compulsive personality disorder in patients with binge eating disorder." *Behaviour Research and Therapy* 42(1) January,57–65.

Gunderson JG, Kolb JE, Austin V (July 1981). "The diagnostic interview for borderline patients." *Am J Psychiatry. 138 (7): 896–903.*

Gunderson, John G. (26 May 2011). "Borderline Personality Disorder." *The New England Journal of Medicine. 364 (21): 2037–2042.*

Gunderson, JG; Sabo, AN (1993). "The phenomenological and conceptual interface between borderline personality disorder and PTSD". *Am J Psychiatry. 150 (1): 19–27.*

Gunderson JG, Elliott GR (March 1985). "The interface between borderline personality disorder and affective disorder." *Am J Psychiatry.* *142 (3): 277–88.*

Gunderson, John G.; Links, Paul S. (2008). *Borderline Personality Disorder: A Clinical Guide (2nd ed.).* American Psychiatric Publishing, Inc.

Guntrip, Harry (1969). *Schizoid Phenomena, Object-Relations, and The Self.* New York: International Universities Press.

Guo, Guang; Ou, Xiao-Ming; Roettger, Michael; Shih, Jean C. (May 2008). "The VNTR 2 repeat in MAOA and delinquent behavior in adolescence and young adulthood: associations and MAOA promoter activity." *European Journal of Human Genetics. Nature Publishing Group. 16 (5): 626–34.*

Guo G, Roettger M, Shih JC (August 2008). "The integration of genetic propensities into social-control models of delinquency and violence among male youths." *American Sociological Review. 73 (4): 543–568.*

Hales E and Yudofsky JA, eds. (2003). *The American Psychiatric Press Textbook of Psychiatry.* Washington, DC: American Psychiatric Publishing, Inc.

Hales, E. (1 February 1996). "Psychopathy and Antisocial Personality Disorder: A Case of Diagnostic Confusion," *Psychiatric Times. UBM Medica. 13 (2).*

Halmi, KA; et al. (December 2005). "The relation among perfectionism, obsessive–compulsive personality disorder, and obsessive–compulsive disorder in individuals with eating disorders." *Int J Eat Disord. 38 (4): 371–4.*

Halpern, L, Trachtman, H. and Duckworth, K. "From Within: A Consumer Perspective on Psychiatric Hospitals," in Textbook of *Hospital Psychiatry*, S. Sharfstein, F. Dickerson and J. Oldham eds. American Psychiatric Publishing, 2009, pp.237-244.

Hands, D. Wade (December 2004). "On Operationalisms and Economics". Journal of Economic Issues. 38 (4): 953–968.

Harbinger, New (May 22, 2013). "Goodbye to the DSM-V". *Huffington Post. Retrieved May 23, 2013.*

Haznedar, M. M.; Buchsbaum, M. S.; Hazlett, E. A.; Shihabuddin, L.; New, A.; Siever, L. J. (2004). "Cingulate gyrus volume and metabolism in the schizophrenia spectrum." *Schizophrenia Research. 71 (2–3): 249–262.*

Healy D (2006) The Latest Mania: Selling Bipolar Disorder *PLoS Med* 3(4): e185.

Heathcoate, Ann (2010). "Eric Berne's Development of Ego State Theory: Where Did It All Begin and Who Influenced Him?". *Transactional Analysis Journal. 40 (3–4): 254–260.*

Herman, Judith Lewis; Judith Herman MD (1992). *Trauma and recovery.* New York: BasicBooks.

Herbert JD, Hope DA, Bellack AS (1992). "Validity of the distinction between generalized social phobia and avoidant personality disorder." *J Abnorm Psychol. 101 (2): 332–9.*

Herpertz SC, Dietrich TM, Wenning B, et al. (August 2001). "Evidence of abnormal amygdala functioning in borderline personality disorder: a functional MRI study." *Biol. Psychiatry. 50 (4): 292–8.*

Hesse M, Schliewe S, Thomsen RR; Schliewe; Thomsen (2005). "Rating of personality disorder features in popular movie characters." *BMC Psychiatry. London: BioMed Central. 5: 45.*

Hill, G. (2001). *A Level Psychology Through Diagrams.* Oxford University Press.

Hinshaw, Stephen P.; Lee, Steve S. (2003). "Conduct and Oppositional Defiant Disorders" (PDF). *In Mash, Eric J.; Barkely, Russell A. Child Psychopathology* (2 ed.). New York: Guilford Press. pp. 144–198.

Hinshelwood RD (March 1999). "The difficult patient. The role of 'scientific psychiatry' in understanding patients with chronic schizophrenia or severe personality disorder." *Br J Psychiatry. 174 (3): 187–90.*

Hirsh JB, Quilty LC, Bagby RM, McMain SF (August 2012). "The relationship between agreeableness and the development of the working alliance in patients with borderline personality disorder." *J. Pers. Disord. 26 (4): 616–27.*

Hoare, Carol Hren (2002). *Erikson on Development in Adulthood: New Insights from the Unpublished Papers.* New York: Oxford University Press.

Hofvander, Björn; Delorme, Richard; Chaste, Pauline; Nydén, Agneta; Wentz, Elisabet; Stahlberg, Ola; Herbrecht, Evelyn; Stopin, Astrid; Anckarsäter, Henrik; Gillberg,

Christopher; et al. (2009). "Psychiatric and psychosocial problems in adults with normal-intelligence autism spectrum disorders." *BMC Psychiatry. 9 (1): 35.*

Holden C (2010). "Psychiatry. APA seeks to overhaul personality disorder diagnoses." *Science. 327 (5971): 1314.*

Horesh N, Sever J, Apter A (July–August 2003). "A comparison of life events between suicidal adolescents with major depression and borderline personality disorder." *Compr Psychiatry. 44 (4): 277–83.*

Horney, Karen (1999). "Resignation: The Appeal of Freedom". In *Neurosis and Human Growth: The Struggle Towards Self-Realization.* Routledge.

Houts A.C. (2000). "Fifty years of psychiatric nomenclature: Reflections on the 1943 War Department Technical Bulletin, Medical 203". *Journal of Clinical Psychology. 56 (7): 935–967.*

"How Using the Dsm Causes Damage: A Client's Report" *Journal of Humanistic Psychology,* Vol. 41, No. 4, 36-56 (2001).

Huizinga, David; Haberstick, Brett C.; Smolen, Andrew; Menard, Scott; Young, Susan E.; Corley, Robin P.; Stallings, Michael C.; Grotpeter, Jennifer; Hewitt, John K. (October 2006). "Childhood Maltreatment, Subsequent Antisocial Behavior, and the Role of Monoamine Oxidase A Genotype." *Biological Psychiatry. 60 (7): 677–683.*

Huppert, Jonathan D.; Strunk, Daniel R.; Ledley, Deborah Roth; Davidson, Jonathan R. T.; Foa, Edna B. (2008). "Generalized social anxiety disorder and avoidant personality disorder: structural analysis and treatment outcome." *Depression and Anxiety. 25 (5): 441–8.*

ICD-9-CM Codes for Selected General Medical Conditions and Medication-Induced Disorders, Appendix G.

ICD-10 Classification of Mental and Behavioural Disorders: *"Blue Book"* (Clinical descriptions and diagnostic guidelines) und "Green Book" (Diagnostic criteria for research)

Ike, Michael. (1998). "Psychotherapy of Obsessive–compulsive Personality". In *Obsessive–Compulsive Disorders: Practical Management. Third edition.* Jenike, Michael et al. (eds.). St. Louis: Mosby.

Insel, Thomas (29 April 2013). "Transforming Diagnosis". Director's Blog. *National Institute of Mental Health.* Retrieved 2013-09-02.

Jamison, Kay R.; Goodwin, Frederick Joseph (1990). *Manic-depressive illness.* Oxford: Oxford University Press.

Jayson, Sharon (12 May 2013). "Books blast new version of psychiatry's bible, the DSM". USA Today. Retrieved 2013-05-21.

Jefferys, Don; Moore, KA (2008). "Pathological hoarding." *Australian Family Physician. 37 (4): 237–41.*

Jenkins, R. L. and S. Glickman (April 1946). "The Schizoid Child." *American Journal of Orthopsychiatry. 16 (2): 255–61.*

Johnson, Stephen M. 1987). *Humanizing the Narcissistic Style.* W.W. Norton.

Johnson, JG; Smailes, EM; Cohen, P; Brown, J; Bernstein, DP (2000). "Associations between four types of childhood neglect and personality disorder symptoms during adolescence and early adulthood: findings of a community-based longitudinal study." *Journal of personality disorders.* *14 (2): 171–87.*

Johnson, J. G.; Cohen, P; Brown, J; Smailes, EM; Bernstein, DP (1999). "Childhood Maltreatment Increases Risk for Personality Disorders During Early Adulthood." *Archives of General Psychiatry. 56 (7): 600–6.*

Joseph, Sonny (1997). "Chapter 3, Schizoid Personality Disorder". Personality Disorders: New Symptom-Focused Drug Therapy. *Psychology Press.*

Joyce, Peter R.; McKenzie, Janice M.; Luty, Suzanne E.; Mulder, Roger T.; Carter, Janet D.; Sullivan, Patrick F.; Cloninger, C. Robert (2003). "Temperament, childhood environment and psychopathology as risk factors for avoidant and borderline personality disorders." *Australian and New Zealand Journal of Psychiatry. 37 (6): 756–64.*

Kamii, C. (1985). *Young Children Reinvent Arithmetic: Implications of Piaget's Theory.* New York: Teachers College Press.

Kantor, M. (1993, revised 2003). *Distancing: A Guide to Avoidance and Avoidant Personality Disorder.* Westport, Conn: Praeger Publishers.

Kay, Jerald et al. (2000). "Obsessive–Compulsive Disorder". In *Psychiatry: Behavioral Science and Clinical Essentials.* Jenike, Michael et al. Philadelphia: W. B. Saunders.

Karterud, Sigmund (September 2011). "Validity aspects of the Diagnostic and Statistical Manual of Mental Disorders, Fourth Edition, narcissistic personality disorder construct." *Comprehensive psychiatry. 52 (5): 517–526.*

Kendell, R.; Jablensky, A (January 2003). "Distinguishing Between the Validity and Utility of Psychiatric Diagnoses". *American Journal of Psychiatry. 160 (1): 4–12.*

Kendler KS, Czajkowski N, Tambs K, et al. (2006). "Dimensional representations of DSM-IV cluster A personality disorders in a population-based sample of Norwegian twins: a multivariate study." *Psychological Medicine 36 (11): 1583–91.*

Kendler Kenneth S.; Muñoz Rodrigo A.; George Murphy M.D. (2009). "The Development of the Feighner Criteria: A Historical Perspective." *Am J Psychiatry. 167: 134–142.*

Kesselring, T. (1999). *Jean Piaget.* München: Beck.

Khalifa, N., Duggan, C., Stoffers, J., Huband, N., Völlm Birgit, A., Ferriter, M., & Lieb, K. (2010). "Pharmacological interventions for antisocial personality disorder." *Cochrane Database of Systematic Reviews,* (8).

Khan, Masud (1974). "The Role of phobic and counterphobic mechanisms and separation anxiety in schizoid character formation." *The Privacy of the Self - Papers on Psychoanalytic Theory and Technique.* New York: International Universities Press.

Kinderman, Peter (20 May 2013). "Explainer: what is the DSM?". The Conversation Australia. *The Conversation Media Group.* Retrieved 2013-05-21.

Kinney, Dennis K.; Richards, Ruth (2001). "Creativity in Offspring of Schizophrenic and Control Parents: An Adoption Study." *Creativity Research Journal. 13 (1): 17–25.*

Kirk, Stuart A.; Kutchins, Herb (1994). "The Myth of the Reliability of DSM". *Journal of Mind and Behavior.* 15 (1&2): 71–86. Archived from the original on 2008-03-07. Retrieved 2008-03-04.

Kitchener, R. (1986). *Piaget's Theory of Knowledge: Genetic Epistemology & Scientific Reason.* New Haven: Yale University Press.

Klein, Melanie (1932). *The Psychoanalysis of Children.* London: Hogarth Press.

Kleinman A (1997). "Triumph or pyrrhic victory? The inclusion of culture in DSM-IV". *Harv Rev Psychiatry.* 4 (6): 343–4.

Kluft, Richard P. (1990). *Incest-Related Syndromes of Adult Psychopathology.* American Psychiatric Pub, Inc.

Kluft, Richard; Goodwin, Jean (1985). *Childhood Antecedents of Multiple Personality Disorder: Credibility Problems in Multiple Personality Disorder Patients and Abused Children.* American Psychiatric Publishing, Inc.

Koenigsberg HW, Harvey PD, Mitropoulou V, et al. (May 2002). "Characterizing affective instability in borderline personality disorder." *Am J Psychiatry. 159 (5): 784–8.*

Korzekwa MI, Dell PF, Links PS, Thabane L, Webb SP (2008). "Estimating the prevalence of borderline personality disorder in psychiatric outpatients using a two-phase procedure." *Compr Psychiatry. 49 (4): 380–6.*

Kraepelin, E. (1906). *Uber Sprachstorungen im Traume.* Leipzig: Engelmann.

Krawitz R (July 2004). "Borderline personality disorder: attitudinal change following training." *Aust N Z J Psychiatry. 38 (7): 554–9.*

Kreisman J, Strauss H (2004). *Sometimes I Act Crazy. Living With Borderline Personality Disorder.* Wiley & Sons.

Kress, Victoria (July 2014). "The Removal of the Multiaxial System in the DSM-5: Implications and Practice Suggestions for Counselors". *The Professional Counselor Journal.* 4 (3): 191–201.

Kretschmer, Ernst (1931). *Physique and Character.* London: Routledge (International Library of Psychology,1999).

Krueger, RF.; Watson, D.; Barlow, DH.; et al. (2005). "Introduction to the Special Section: Toward a Dimensionally Based Taxonomy of Psychopathology". *Journal of Abnormal Psychology.* 114 (4): 491–493.

Kupfer, David and D. A. Regier (2011). "DSM-V Task Force Member Disclosure Report: David J Kupfer, MD" (PDF). American Psychiatric Association. and "DSM-V Task Force Member Disclosure Report: Darrel Alvin Regier M.D" (PDF). American Psychiatric Association. May 2, 2011. Retrieved May 5, 2011.

Kupfer, David; Regier, Darrell, eds. (2013). *Diagnostic and Statistical Manual of Mental Disorders (5 ed.).* Washington, DC: American Psychiatric Association.

Laing, R. D. (1965). "The Inner Self in the Schizoid Condition". The Divided Self: an Existential Study," in *Sanity and Madness*. Harmondsworth, Middlesex; Baltimore: Penguin Books.

Lane, Christopher. *"The NIMH Withdraws Support for DSM-5". Psychology Today.*

Lane, Christopher (2007). *Shyness: How Normal Behavior Became a Sickness.* Yale University Press. p. 263.

Lane, Christopher (July 24, 2009). "The Diagnostic Madness of DSM-V". *Slate.*

Lazzaretti, Matteo; Morandotti, Niccolò; Sala, Michela; Isola, Miriam; Frangou, Sophia; De Vidovich, Giulia; Marraffini, Elisa; Gambini, Francesca; et al. (2012). "Impaired working memory and normal sustained attention in borderline personality disorder." *Acta Neuropsychiatrica. 24 (6): 349–55.*

Lehnhardt, Fritz-Georg, Astrid Gawronski, Kathleen Pfeiffer, Hanna Kockler, Leonhard Schilbach, and Kai Vogeley (2013). "The investigation and differential diagnosis of Asperger syndrome in adults." *Deutsches Ärzteblatt International. 110 (45): 760.*

Leichsenring, F; Leibing, E; Kruse, J; New, AS; Leweke, F (1 January 2011). "Borderline personality disorder." *Lancet (London, England). 377 (9759): 74–84.*

Lenzenweger, Mark F.; Clarkin, John F. (2005). *Major Theories of Personality Disorder.* Guilford Press.

Levy KN, Meehan KB, Weber M, Reynoso J, Clarkin JF (2005). "Attachment and borderline personality disorder: implications for psychotherapy." *Psychopathology. 38 (2): 64–74.*

Lieb K, Zanarini MC, Schmahl C, Linehan MM, Bohus M (2004). "Borderline personality disorder." *Lancet. 364 (9432): 453–61.*

Lillard, Angeline (2005). *Montessori: The Science Behind the Genius.* New York: Oxford University Press.

Linehan MM, Comtois KA, Murray AM, et al. (July 2006). "Two-year randomized controlled trial and follow-up of dialectical behavior therapy vs therapy by experts for suicidal behaviors and borderline personality disorder." *Arch. Gen. Psychiatry. 63 (7): 757–66.*

Links, Paul S.; Shah, Ravi; Eynan, Rahel (2017). "Psychotherapy for Borderline Personality Disorder: Progress and Remaining Challenges." *Current Psychiatry Reports. 19 (3): 16.*

Lock, M. P. (2008). "Treatment of antisocial personality disorder." *The British Journal of Psychiatry. 193 (5): 426.*

Loeber, Rolf; Keenan, Kate; Lahey, Benjamin B.; Green, Stephanie M.; Thomas, Christopher (August 1993). "Evidence for developmentally based diagnoses of oppositional defiant disorder and conduct disorder." *Journal of Abnormal Child Psychology. International Society for Research in Child and Adolescent Psychopathology. 21 (4): 377–410.*

Livesley, John W. (2001). *Handbook of Personality Disorders: Theory, Research, and Treatment.* The Guilford Press.

Lubke, GH; Laurin, C; Amin, N; Hottenga, JJ; Willemsen, G; van Grootheest, G; Abdellaoui, A; Karssen, LC; Oostra, BA; van Duijn, CM; Penninx, BW; Boomsma, DI (August 2014). "Genome-wide analyses of borderline personality features.." *Molecular Psychiatry. 19 (8): 923–9.*

Lynskey, Michael T.; Fergusson, David M. (June 1995). "Childhood conduct problems, attention deficit behaviors, and adolescent alcohol, tobacco, and illicit drug use." *Journal of Abnormal Child Psychology. International Society for Research in Child and Adolescent Psychopathology. 23 (3): 281–302.*

MacFarlane, Malcolm M. (ed.) (2004). *Family Treatment of Personality Disorders. Advances in Clinical Practice.* Binghamton, NY: The Haworth Press.

Mackinnon DF, Pies R (February 2006). "Affective instability as rapid cycling: theoretical and clinical implications for borderline personality and bipolar spectrum disorders." *Bipolar Disord. 8 (1): 1–14.*

MacManus, Deirdre; Fahy, Tom (August 2008). "Personality disorders." *Medicine 36 (8): 436–441.*

Magnavita, Jeffrey J. (1997). Restructuring Personality Disorders: A Short-Term Dynamic Approach. *New York: The Guilford Press.*

Maher, Alicia R. (June 2012). "Summary of the comparative effectiveness review on off-label use of atypical antipsychotics". *J Manag Care Pharm.* 18 (5 Suppl B): S1–20.

Manfiel Maj, Mario (2005). *Personality Disorders.* Chichester: J. Wiley & Sons.

Maj, Mario (2005). *Personality Disorders.* Chichester: J. Wiley & Sons.

Manfield, Philip (1992). *Split Self/Split Object: Understanding and Treating Borderline, Narcissistic, and Schizoid Disorders. N.Y.:* Jason Aronson.

Martens, Willem H. J. (2010). "Schizoid personality disorder linked to unbearable and inescapable loneliness." *The European Journal of Psychiatry. 24 (1).*

Maser, JD. & Patterson, T. (2002). "Spectrum and nosology: implications for DSM-5." *Psychiatric Clinics of North America*, December, 25(4)p855-885.

Maser, JD & Akiskal, HS. et al. (2002). "Spectrum concepts in major mental disorders." *Psychiatric Clinics of North America,* Vol. 25, Special issue 4.

Masterson, James F. and Ralph Klein (1995). *Disorders of the Self - The Masterson Approach.* New York: Brunner / Mazel.

Mather, Amber A. (2008). "Associations Between Body Weight and Personality Disorders in a Nationally Representative Sample." *Psychosomatic Medicine. 70 (9): 1012–1019.*

Matsui M., Sumiyoshi T., Kato K.; et al. (2004). "Neuropsychological profile in patients with schizotypal personality disorder or schizophrenia." *Psychological Reports. 94 (2): 387–397.*

May F, Chen Q, Gilbertson M, Shenton M, Pitman R (2004). "Cavum septum pellucidum in monozygotic twins discordant for combat exposure: relationship to posttraumatic stress disorder." *Biol. Psychiatry. 55 (6): 656–8.*

Mayes, Rick; Bagwell, Catherine; Erkulwater, Jennifer L. (2009). "The Transformation of Mental Disorders in the 1980s: The DSM-III, Managed Care," and "Cosmetic Psychopharmacology"". *Medicating Children: ADHD and Pediatric Mental Health.* Harvard University Press.

Mayo Clinic Staff (2 April 2016). "Overview- Antisocial personality disorder". *Mayo Clinic.*

McCommon, B. (2006). "Antipsychiatry and the Gay Rights Movement." *Psychiatr Serv* 57:1809, December.

McGlashan T.H., Grilo C.M., Skodol A.E., Gunderson J.G., Shea M.T., Morey L.C.; et al. (2000). "The collaborative longitudinal personality disorders study: Baseline axis I/II and II/II diagnostic co-occurrence." *Acta Psychiatrica Scandinavica. 102: 256–264.*

McHugh Paul R (2005). "Striving for Coherence: Psychiatry's Efforts Over Classification". *JAMA.* 293 (20): 2526–2528.

McNally, RJ (March 2001). "On Wakefield's harmful dysfunction analysis of mental disorder". *Behaviour Research and Therapy.* 39 (3): 309–14.

McWilliams, Nancy (2011). *Psychoanalytic Diagnosis: Understanding Personality Structure in the Clinical Process (2nd ed.)*. New York: Guilford Press.

Mellsop, Graham (1973). "Antecedents of Schizophrenia." *Australian and New Zealand Journal of Psychiatry 7 (3): 208–211*.

Menelaos L. Batrinos (2012). "Testosterone and Aggressive Behavior in Man." *Int J Endocrinol Metab. 10 (3): 563–568*.

Messerly, J.G. (1992). *Piaget's Conception of Evolution: Beyond Darwin and Lamarck*. Lanham, MD: Rowman & Littlefield.

Mezzich, Juan E. (2002). "International Surveys on the Use of ICD-10 and Related Diagnostic Systems" (guest editorial, abstract). *Psychopathology*. 35 (2–3): 72–75.

Miller AL, Muehlenkamp JJ, Jacobson CM (July 2008). "Fact or fiction: diagnosing borderline personality disorder in adolescents." Clin Psychol Rev. 28 (6): 969–81.

Millon, Theodore (1981). *Disorders of Personality: DSM-III, Axis II*. New York: Wiley.

Millon, Theodore (2004). *Personality Disorders in Modern Life*. John Wiley & Sons, Inc., Hoboken, New Jersey.

Millon, Theodore; Martinez, Alexandra (1995). "Avoidant Personality Disorder." *In Livesley, W. John. The DSM-IV Personality Disorders*. Guilford Press.

Millon, Theodore (2004). *The Schizoid Personality (Chapter 11).* In: *Personality Disorders in Modern Life.* Wiley, 2nd Edition.

Millon, Theodore; Davis, Roger Dale (1996). *Disorders of Personality: DSM-IV and Beyond.* New York: Wiley.

Millon, Theodore; Millon, Carrie M.; Meagher, Sarah; Grossman, Seth; Ramnath, Rowena (2004). *Personality Disorders in Modern Life.* Wiley.

Moffitt, Terrie E. (October 1993). "Adolescence-limited and life-course-persistent antisocial behavior: A developmental taxonomy." *Psychological Review. American Psychological Association. 100 (4): 674–701.*

Montessori, Maria (1948). *The Discovery of the Child.* Madras: Kalkshetra Publications Press.

Montessori, Maria (1949). *The Absorbent Mind.* Madras: Theosophical Publishing House.

Montessori, Maria (1914). *Dr. Montessori's Own Handbook.* New York: Frederick A. Stokes Company.

Montessori, Maria (1912). *The Montessori Method.* New York: Frederick A. Stokes Company.

Montessori, Maria (1936). *The Secret of Childhood.* New York: Longmans, Green.

Moore TM, Scarpa A, Raine A (2002). "A meta-analysis of serotonin metabolite 5-HIAA and antisocial behavior." *Aggressive Behavior. 28 (4): 299–316.*

Morgan, John H. (2019). *An Encyclopedic Dictionary of Interpersonal Psychotherapy: Concepts and Terms* (Elkhart, IN: MacBain & Boyd, Publishers).

Morgan, John H. (2019). *Child Psychopathology in Clinical Practice: The Psychoanalytic Theories of Karen Horney, Melanie Klein, and Anna Freud* (Elkhart, IN: MacBain & Boyd, Publishers).

Morgan, John H. (2018). *Psychopathology: A Clinical Guide to Personality Disorders.* South Bend, IN: GTF Books.

Morgan, John H. (2017a). "Geriatric Narcissism: The Psychotherapeutics of Self-Regard among the Elderly (a literature review)," Chapter 12 in John H. Morgan, *Geriatric Psychotherapy: Essays in Clinical Studies and Counseling Psychology* (Mishawaka, IN: GTF Books, 2017).

Morgan, John H. (2017b). "Geriatric Health and Social Values: Exploring the Practical Range of Sociopharmacology (with particular attention to health care practices among the eldery), Chapter 8 in John H. Morgan, *Geriatric Psychotherapy: Essays in Clinical Studies and Counseling Psychology* (Mishawaka, IN: GTF Books, 2017).

Morgan, John H. (2017c, 2nd edition). *Clinical Psychotherapy: A History of Theory and Practice (from Sigmund Freud to Aaron Beck).* South Bend, IN: GTF Books.

Morgan, John H. (2016). *Clinical Psychotherapy: A History of Theory and Practice (from Sigmund Freud to Aaron Beck).* South Bend, IN: GTF Books.

Morgan, John H. (2015a). "Palliative Psychotherapy in the

Treatment of Geriatric Depression: A Review of Evidence-Based Psychogenic Options," *Innovative Issues and Approaches in Social Sciences* (Vol. 8, No. 1:46-59, 2015).

Morgan, John H. (2015b). "Cognitive Behavioral Therapy and Reminiscence Therapy in the Treatment of Depression: A Convergent Palliative Care Methodology in Geriatric Psychotherapy," *The Online Journal of Counseling and Education* 2015, 4(2):51-67.

Morgan, John H. (2014a). "The Interpersonal Psychotherapy of Harry Stack Sullivan: Remembering the Legacy," *Journal of Psychology and Psychotherapy* (Volume 4, Issue 6, 2014).

Morgan, John H. (2014b). "The Deep Structure of Human Nature: Probing the Psycho-Social Propensities in Behavioral Matrices (with special reference to E. O. Wilson)," *Journal of Academic Emergency Medicine Case Reports* / Akademik A;Oct, 2014, Vol. 5 Issue 10, p112.

Morgan, John H. (2013a). "What to Do When There is Nothing to Do: The Psychotherapeutic Value of Meaning Therapy in the Treatment of Late Life Depression," *Health, Culture and Society,* Vol. 5, #1 (2013), pp.52-59.

Morgan, John H. (2013b)."Late-Life Depression and the Counseling Agenda: Exploring Geriatric Logotherapy as a Treatment Modality," *International Journal of Psychological Research*, Vol. VI, #1 (2013).

Morgan, John H. (2012a). "The Personal Meaning of Social Values in the Work of Abraham Maslow," *Interpersona: International Journal of Interpersonal Relationships Vol. 6* (1) June, 2012: 1-19.

Morgan, John H. (2012b). "Geriatric Logotherapy: Exploring the Psychotherapeutics of Memory in Treating the Elderly," *Psychological Thought, Vol. 5, #2*, 2012:99-105.

Morgan, John H. (2012c). "Pastoral Nurture of the Elderly: The 'Happy Memory' in Geriatric Logotherapy"in *Clinical Pastoral Psychotherapy: A Practitioner's Handbook for Ministry Professionals* Expanded 2nd Edition (Mishawaka, IN: GTF Books, 2012).

Morgan, John H. (2012d). "Medication and Counseling in Psychiatric Practice: Biogenic Psychopharmacology and Psychogenic Psychotherapy (Partnering in the Treatment of Mental Illness)," in *Clinical Pastoral Psychotherapy: A Practitioner's Handbook for Ministry Professionals* (Expanded 2nd Edition, Mishawaka, IN: GTF Books, 2012).

Morgan, John H. (2012e). "A Tribute to Carl Rogers," in *Clinical Pastoral Psychotherapy: A Practitioner's Handbook for Ministry Professionals* Expanded 2nd Edition (Mishawaka, IN: GTF Books, 2012).

Morgan, John H. (2011). "*On Becoming a Person* (1961) Carl Rogers' Celebrated Classic in Memoriam," *Journal of Psychological Issues in Organizational Culture* (II, #3, 95-105, Oct. 2011).

Morgan, John H. (2010). "Harry Stack Sullivan and Interpersonal Psychotherapy: The Father of Modern Social Psychiatry," in *Foundation Theology 2010* (Mishawaka, IN: GTF Books). .

Morgan, John H. (2006). "Personal Meaning as Psychotherapy: The Interpretive Hermeneutic of Viktor Frankl," In *Foundation Theology 2006* (Mishawaka, IN: GTF Books).

Morgan, John H. (1983). "Personal Meaning as Therapy: The Roots and Branches of Frankl's Psychology," *Pastoral Psychology*, Fall Issue, 1983.

Morgan, John H. (1978). "The Theology of Medicine: The Political-Philosophical Foundations of Medical Ethics," *Journal of the American Academy of Religion,* Vol. 46, #2, pp. 250ff., 1978.

Morgan, John H. (1976). "Pastoral Ecstasy and the Authentic Self: Theological Meanings in Symbolic Distance," *Pastoral Psychology*, XXV, #2 (Winter, 1976), 128-137.

Morgan, John H. (1975). "Silence as Creative Therapy: A Contemplative Approach to Pastoral Care," *Journal of Pastoral Care*, XXIX, 4 (Dec., 1975): 248-253.

Morgan, John H. (1973). "The Psychotherapeutics of Silence," *Spiritual Frontiers*, V, #2 (Spring, 1973).

Murphy, Dominic; Stich, Stephen (16 December 1998). "Darwin in the Madhouse: Evolutionary Psychology and the Classification of Mental Disorders". Archived from the original on 5 December 2013. Retrieved 2013-12-03.

Murphy, Michael; Cowan, Ronald; Sederer, Lloyd I., eds. (2009). "Personality Disorders." *Blueprints Psychiatry (5th ed.).* Wolters Kluwer/Lippincott Williams & Wilkins.

Murray, Robin M. et al (2008). *Psychiatry. Fourth Edition.* Cambridge University Press.

Nannarello, Joseph J. (1953). "Schizoid." *The Journal of Nervous and Mental Disease. 118 (3): 237–249.*

Nedic, Aleksandra; Zivanovic, Olga; Lisulov, Ratomir (2011). "Nosological status of social phobia: contrasting classical and recent literature." *Current Opinion in Psychiatry. 24 (1): 61–6.*

Nehls N (1998). "Borderline personality disorder: gender stereotypes, stigma, and limited system of care." *Issues Ment Health Nurs. 19 (2): 97–112.*

Nehls N (August 1999). "Borderline personality disorder: the voice of patients." *Res Nurs Health. 22 (4): 285–93.*

Nenadic, Igor; Güllmar, Daniel; Dietzek, Maren; Langbein, Kerstin; Steinke, Johanna; Gader, Christian (February 2015). "Brain structure in narcissistic personality disorder: A VBM and DTI pilot study." *Psychiatry Research Neuroimaging. Elsevier Ireland. 231 (2): 184–186.*

Netherton, S.D.; Holmes, D.; Walker, C.E. (1999). *Child and Adolescent Psychological Disorders: Comprehensive Textbook.* New York, NY: Oxford University Press.

New, Antonia; Triebwasser Joseph; Charney Dennis (October 2008). "The case for shifting borderline personality disorder to Axis I" (PDF). *Biol. Psychiatry. 64 (8): 653–9.*

Newman, Barbara M.; Newman, P. R. (2011). *Development Through Life : A Psychosocial Approach.* Belmont, CA: Wadsworth Cengage Learning.

Nolen-Hoeksema, S. (2014). "Personality Disorders. (pp. 266–267)." *Abnormal Psychology* (6th ed.). New York, NY: McGraw-Hill.

Nordgaard, Julie; Louis A. Sass (June 2013). "The psychiatric interview: validity, structure, and subjectivity". European archives of *Psychiatry and Clinical Neuroscience.* 263 (4): 353–364.

Nussbaum, Abraham (2013). The Pocket Guide to the DSM-5 Diagnostic Exam. *Arlington: American Psychiatric Association.*

Oaklander, Violet. (2006). *Hidden Treasure : A Map to the Child's Inner Self.* London, Karnac Books.

O'Donohue, William (2007). *Personality Disorders : Toward the DSM-V.* Los Angeles: SAGE Publications.

Oldham, John M.; Morris, Lois B. (1990). *The Personality Self-portrait: Why You Think, Work, Love, and Act the Way You Do.* Bantam.

Oldham, John M., Skodol, Andrew E., Bender, Donna S. (2005) *The American Psychiatric Publishing Textbook of Personality Disorders.* American Psychiatric Publishing.

Oldham, John M., Skodol, Andrew E., Bender, Donna S. (2005). *Textbook of Personality Disorders.* American Psychiatric Publishing.

Oldham, John M. (2005). "Personality Disorders". *FOCUS.* 3: 372–382.

O'Neil, Aisling; Thomas Frodl (18 January 2012). "Brain structure and function in borderline personality disorder." *Brain Structure and Function. 217: 767–782.*

Osborne, Duncan (May 15, 2008). "Flap Flares Over Gender Diagnosis". *Gay City News. Archived from the original on October 24, 2008. Retrieved June 14, 2008.*

Oscar-Berman M; Valmas M; Sawyer K; Kirkley S; Gansler D; Merritt D; Couture A (April 2009). "Frontal brain dysfunction in alcoholism with and without antisocial personality disorder." *Neuropsychiatric Disease and Treatment. 5: 309–326.*

Oumaya, M; Friedman, S; Pham, A; Abou Abdallah, T; Guelfi, JD; Rouillon, F (October 2008). "[Borderline personality disorder, self-mutilation and suicide: literature review]." *L'Encephale. 34 (5): 452–8.*

Overholser, J. C. (November 1989). "Differentiation between schizoid and avoidant personalities: an empirical test". *Canadian Journal of Psychiatry. 34 (8): 785–90.*

Panagiotis, Parpottas (2012). "A critique on the use of standard psychopathological classifications in understanding human distress: The example of 'Schizoid Personality Disorder'." *Counselling Psychology Review 27 (1): 44–52.*

Parens, Henri (2014). *War Is Not Inevitable: On the Psychology of War and Aggression.* Lexington Books.

Paris, Joel (2014). "Modernity and narcissistic personality disorder." *Personality Disorders: Theory, Research, and Treatment, 5 (2): 220.*

Paris J (2008). *Treatment of Borderline Personality Disorder. A Guide to Evidence-Based Practice.* The Guilford Press.

Paris J (2004). "Borderline or bipolar? Distinguishing borderline personality disorder from bipolar spectrum disorders." *Harv Rev Psychiatry.* 12 (3): 140–5.

Paris J (June 2004). "Is hospitalization useful for suicidal patients with borderline personality disorder?". *J. Pers. Disord.* 18 (3): 240–7.

Paris J (February 2010). "Effectiveness of different psychotherapy approaches in the treatment of borderline personality disorder." *Curr Psychiatry Rep.* 12 (1): 56–60.

Parker, AG; Boldero, JM; Bell, RC (September 2006). "Borderline personality disorder features: the role of self-discrepancies and self-complexity." *Psychol Psychother.* 79 (Pt 3): 309–21.

Patrick, Christopher J. (2005). *Handbook of Psychopathy.* Guilford Press.

Pearson, Catherine (20 May 2013). "DSM-5 Changes: What Parents Need To Know About The First Major Revision In Nearly 20 Years". *The Huffington Post.* Retrieved 2013-05-21.

Penzel, Fred. (2000). *Obsessive–Compulsive Disorders: A Complete Guide to Getting Well and Staying Well.* Oxford University Press, USA.

Perry, J. C. (1996). "Dependent personality disorder." In *Gabbard, Glen O.; Atkinson, Sarah D. Synopsis of Treatments of Psychiatric Disorders. American Psychiatric Press. pp. 995–8.*

Phillips, James; Frances, Allen; Cerullo, Michael A; Chardavoyne, John; Decker, Hannah S; First, Michael B; Ghaemi, Nassir; Greenberg, Gary; et al. (January 13, 2012). "The Six Most Essential Questions in Psychiatric Diagnosis: A Pluralogue. Part 1: Conceptual and Definitional Issues in Psychiatric Diagnosis" (PDF). Philosophy, Ethics, and Humanities in Medicine. *BioMed Central.* 7 (3): 1–51.

Piaget, Jean (1926). *The Language and Thought of the Child.* London: Routledge & Kegan Paul.

Piaget, Jean (1928). *The Child's Conception of the World.* London: Routledge and Kegan Paul.

Piaget, Jean (1932). *The Moral Judgment of the Child.* London: Kegan Paul, Trench, Trubner and Co.

Piaget, Jean (1952). *The Origins of Intelligence in Children.* New York: International University Press.

Piaget, Jean (1951). *The Psychology of Intelligence.* London: Routledge and Kegan Paul.

Piaget, Jean (1955). *The Child's Construction of Reality.* London: Routledge and Kegan Paul.

Piaget, Jean (1964). *The Early Growth of Logic in the Child.* London: Routledge and Kegan Paul.

Piaget, Jean (1971). *Genetic Epistemology.* New York: W.W. Norton.

Piaget, Jean (1972). *The Principles of Genetic Epistemology.* New York: Basic Books.

Piaget, Jean (1970). *Science of Education and the Psychology of the Child.* New York: Orion Press.

Piaget, Jean (1977). *The Grasp of Consciousness: Action and Concept in the Young Child.* London: Routledge and Kegan Paul.

Piaget, Jean (1972). *Psychology and Epistemology: Towards a Theory of Knowledge.* Harmondsworth, UK: Penguin.

Piaget, Jean (1977). Gruber, H.E.; Voneche, J.J., eds. *The Essential Piaget.* New York: Basic Books.

Pilkonis PA, Frank E (1988). "Personality pathology in recurrent depression: nature, prevalence, and relationship to treatment response." *Am J Psychiatry. 145: 435–41.*

Pincus AL, Ansell EB, Pimentel CA, Cain NM, Wright AG, Levy KN; Ansell; Pimentel; Cain; Wright; Levy (2009). "Initial construction and validation of the Pathological Narcissism Inventory." *Psychol Assess. 21 (3): 365–79.*

Pincus, H. A.; Zarin, DA; First, M (1998). "'Clinical Significance' and DSM-IV". *Arch Gen Psychiatry.* 55 (12): 1145; author reply 1147–8.

Pinkofsky, HB (1997). "Mnemonics for DSM-IV personality disorders." *Psychiatric Services. Washington, D.C. 48 (9): 1197–8.*

Pinto, Anthony (2014). "Capacity to Delay Reward Differentiates Obsessive-Compulsive Disorder and Obsessive-Compulsive Personality Disorder." *Biol Psychiatry. 75 (8): 653–659.*

Pinto, Anthon y; Eisen, Jane L.; Mancebo, Maria C.; Rasmussen, Steven A. (2008). "Obsessive-Compulsive Personality Disorder." In Abramowitz, Jonathan S.; McKay, Dean; Taylor, Steven. *Obsessive-Compulsive Disorder: Subtypes and Spectrum Conditions. Elsevier. pp. 246–263.*

Poland, JS. (2001) Review of Volume 1 of DSM-IV sourcebook Archived May 1, 2005, at the *Wayback Machine.*

Poland, JS. (2001) Review of vol 2 of DSM-IV sourcebook Archived September 27, 2007, at the *Wayback Machine.*

Posner MI, Tang YY, Lynch G (2014). "Mechanisms of white matter change induced by meditation training." *Frontiers in Psychology. 5 (1220): 297–302.*

"Professor co-authors letter about America's mental health manual". *Point Park University.* Retrieved 6 February 2017.

"Professor co-authors letter about America's mental health manual". *Point Park University.* December 12, 2011.

Pulay, A. J., Stinson, F. S., Dawson, D. A., Goldstein, R. B., Chou, S. P., Huang, B.; et al. (2009). "Prevalence, correlates, disability, and comorbidity of DSM-IV schizotypal personality disorder: results from the wave 2 national epidemiologic survey on alcohol and related conditions." *Primary Care Companion to the Journal of Clinical Psychiatry. 11 (2): 53–67.*

Quadrio, C (December 2005). "Axis One/Axis Two: A disordered borderline." *Australian and New Zealand Journal of Psychiatry. 39: A107.*

Raine, A. (2006). "Schizotypal personality: Neurodevelopmental and psychosocial trajectories." *Annual Review of Psychology. 2: 291–326.*

Raine, Adrian; Lydia Lee; Yaling Yang; Patrick Colletti (2010). "Neurodevelopmental marker for limbic maldevelopment in antisocial personality disorder and psychopathy." *BJPsych. the British Journal of Psychiatry. 197 (3): 186–192.*

Raja M, Azzoni A (2007). "The impact of obsessive–compulsive personality disorder on the suicidal risk of patients with mood disorders." *Psychopathology. 40 (3): 184–90.*

Ralevski, E.; Sanislow, C. A.; Grilo, C. M.; Skodol, A. E.; Gunderson, J. G.; Tracie Shea, M.; Yen, S.; Bender, D. S.; et al. (2005). "Avoidant personality disorder and social phobia: distinct enough to be separate disorders?." *Acta Psychiatrica Scandinavica. 112 (3): 208–14.*

Rapkin, AJ; Lewis, EI (November 2013). *"Treatment of premenstrual dysphoric disorder."* Womens Health (Lond Engl). 9 (6): 537–56.

Rautiainen, M.-R.; Paunio, T.; Repo-Tiihonen, E.; Virkkunen, M.; Ollila, H. M.; Sulkava, S.; Jolanki, O.; Palotie, A.; Tiihonen, J. (6 September 2016). "Genome-wide association study of antisocial personality disorder." *Translational Psychiatry. Macmillian Publishers Limited. 6 (9): e883.*

Reber, Arthur S. (2009) [1985]. *The Penguin Dictionary of Psychology (4th ed.).* London; New York: Penguin Books.

Reichborn-Kjennerud, Ted (1 March 2010). "The genetic epidemiology of personality disorders." *Dialogues in Clinical Neuroscience. 12 (1): 103–114.*

Reichborn-Kjennerud, T.; Czajkowski, N.; Torgersen, S.; Neale, M. C.; Orstavik, R. E.; Tambs, K.; Kendler, K. S. (2007). "The Relationship Between Avoidant Personality Disorder and Social Phobia: A Population-Based Twin Study." *American Journal of Psychiatry. 164 (11): 1722–8.*

Retzlaff, P. D. (1995*). Tactical Psychotherapy of the Personality Disorders: An MCMI-III-Based Approach.* Boston: Allyn & Bacon.

Reich, James (2009). "Avoidant personality disorder and its relationship to social phobia." *Current Psychiatry Reports. 11 (1): 89–93.*

Rheaume, J; Freeston, MH; Dugas, MJ; Letarte, H; Ladouceur, R (1995). "Perfectionism, responsibility and obsessive-compulsive symptoms." *Behav Res Ther. 33. 33 (7): 785–794.*

Richards, Henry Jay (1993). *Therapy of the Substance Abuse Syndromes.* New York: Jason Aronson.

Rissmiller, DJ, D.O., Rissmiller, J. (2006) "Letter in reply." *Psychiatr Serv* 57:1809-a-1810, December.

Roazen, Paul (1976). Erik H. Erikson: The Power and Limits of a Vision. New York: Free Press.

Roazen, Paul (1993). "Erik H. Erikson as a Teacher". *The Psychohistory Review. 22 (1): 101–117.*

Robinson, David J. (2005). *Disordered Personalities.* Rapid Psychler Press.

Robinson, David J. (1999). *The Field Guide to Personality Disorders.* Rapid Psychler Press.

Robinson, David J. (2003). *Reel Psychiatry: Movie Portrayals of Psychiatric Conditions.* Port Huron, Michigan: Rapid Psychler Press.

Ronningstam, Elsa (2016). "New Insights Into Narcissistic Personality Disorder." *Psychiatric Times, 33 (2): 11.*

Ronningstam, Elsa (19 January 2016). "Pathological Narcissism and Narcissistic Personality Disorder: Recent Research and Clinical Implications." *Current Behavioral Neuroscience Reports. Springer International Publishing. 3 (1): 34–42.*

Ronningstam E (2010). "Narcissistic personality disorder: a current review." *Curr Psychiatry Rep. 12 (1): 68–75.*

Rosenthal, MZ; Cheavens, JS; Lejuez, CW; Lynch, TR (September 2005). "Thought suppression mediates the relationship between negative affect and borderline personality disorder symptoms." *Behav Res There. 43 (9): 1173–85.*

Rossi A; et al. (2000). "Pattern of comorbidity among anxious and odd personality disorders: the case of obsessive–compulsive personality disorder." *CNS Spectr. 5 (9): 23–6.*

Ruocco, Anthony C.; Amirthavasagam, Sathya, Choi-Kain, Lois W.; McMain, Shelley F. (2013). "Neural Correlates of Negative Emotionality in Borderline Personality Disorder:

An Activation-Likelihood-Estimation Meta-Analysis." *Biological Psychiatry. 73 (2): 153–160.*

Rydén, Göran; Rydén, Eleonore; Hetta, Jerker (2008). "Borderline personality disorder and autism spectrum disorder in females: A cross-sectional study." *Clinical Neuropsychiatry. 5 (1): 22–30.*

Ryle, A. & Kerr, I. B. (2002). *Introducing Cognitive Analytic Therapy: Principles and Practice.* Chichester: John Wiley & Sons.

Sachdeva S.; Goldman G.; Mustata G.; Deranja E.; Gregory R. J. (2013). "Naturalistic outcomes of evidence-based therapies for borderline personality disorder at a university clinic: A quasi-randomized trial." *Journal of the American Psychoanalytic Association. 61: 578–584.*

Sachse S, Keville S, Feigenbaum J (Jun 2011). "A feasibility study of mindfulness-based cognitive therapy for individuals with borderline personality disorder." *Psychology and Psychotherapy. 84 (2): 184–200.*

Sadock, Benjamin J. (October 1999). "DSM-IV Sourcebook, vol. 4 (Book Forum: Assessment and Diagnosis)". *American Journal of Psychiatry. 156 (10): 1655.*

Salekin, R. (2002). "Psychopathy and therapeutic pessimism: Clinical lore or clinical reality?." *Clinical Psychology Review. 22: 169–183.*

Salzman, Leon. (1995).*Treatment of Obsessive and Compulsive Behaviors*, Jason Aronson Publishers.

Samuels J et al. (2000). "Personality disorders and normal personality dimensions in obsessive–compulsive disorder." *Br J Psychiatry*. Nov. 177: 457–62.

Samuels, Jack; Costa, Paul T. (2012). "Obsessive-Compulsive Personality Disorder." In Widiger, Thomas. *The Oxford Handbook of Personality Disorders. Oxford University Press. p. 568.*

Sansone, Randy A.; Sansone, Lori A. (1 May 2011). "Gender Patterns in Borderline Personality Disorder." *Innovations in Clinical Neuroscience. 8 (5): 16–20.*

Sansone, R.A.; Hendricks, C. M.; Gaither, G. A.; Reddington, A. (2004). "Prevalence of anxiety symptoms among a sample of outpatients in an internal medicine clinic: a pilot study." *Depress Anxiety. 19. 19 (2): 133–136.*

Sansone, R.A.; Hendricks, C. M.; Sellbom, M.; Reddington, A. (2003). "Anxiety symptoms and healthcare utilization among a sample of outpatients in an internal medicine clinic." *Int J Psychiatry Med. 33. 33 (2): 133–139.*

Sauer, SE; Baer, Ruth A.; Baer, RA (February 2009). "Relationships between thought suppression and symptoms of borderline personality disorder." *J. Pers. Disord. 23 (1): 48–61.*

Sciencedaily.com (2008). "Possible Genetic Causes Of Borderline Personality Disorder Identified." 20 December.

Schaffer, David (1996). "A Participant's Observations: Preparing DSM-IV" (PDF). *Can J Psychiatry.* 41: 325–329.

Schatzberg, Alan and Francis (2010). Psychiatrists Propose Revisions to Diagnosis Manual. via *PBS Newshour,* interview February 10.

Schmahl CG, Elzinga BM, Vermetten E, Sanislow C, McGlashan TH, Bremner JD (July 2003). "Neural correlates of memories of abandonment in women with and without borderline personality disorder." *Biol. Psychiatry. 54 (2): 142–51.*

Schuldberg, David (2001). "Six subclinical spectrum traits in normal creativity." *Creativity Research Journal. 13 (1): 5–16.*

Schulze L, Dziobek I, Vater A, Heekeren HR, Bajbouj M, Renneberg B, Heuser I, Roepke S; Dziobek; Vater; Heekeren; Bajbouj; Renneberg; Heuser; Roepke (2013). "Gray matter abnormalities in patients with narcissistic personality disorder." *J Psychiatr Res. 47 (10): 1363–9.*

Scoriels, Linda (2013). "Modafinil effects on cognition and emotion in schizophrenia and its neurochemical modulation in the brain." *Neuropharmacology. 64: 168–184.*

Sederer, Lloyd I. (2009). *Blueprints Psychiatry (5th ed.).* Philadelphia: Wolters Kluwer/Lippincott Williams & Wilkins.

Seinfeld, Jeffrey (1991): *The Empty Core: An Object Relations Approach to Psychotherapy of the Schizoid Personality.* Jason Aronson.

Selby EA (October 2013). "Chronic sleep disturbances and borderline personality disorder symptoms." *J Consult Clin Psychol. 81 (5): 941–7.*

Seligman, Martin E.P. (1984). "Chapter 11." *Abnormal Psychology.* W. W. Norton & Company.

Semple, David; Smyth, Roger; Burns, Jonathan; Darjee, Rajan; McIntosh, Andrew (2005). *The Oxford Handbook of Psychiatry.* New York: Oxford University Press.

Shaffer, David R. (2009). *Social and Personality Development (6th ed.).* Australia: Wadsworth.

Sharfstein, SS. (2005) "Big Pharma and American Psychiatry: The Good, the Bad, and the Ugly" *Psychiatric News* August 19, 2005 Volume 40 Number 16.

Shea MT; et al. (1992). "Comorbidity of personality disorders and depression; implications for treatment." *J Consult Clin Psychol. 60: 857–68.*

Shedler J, Beck A, Fonagy P, Gabbard GO, Gunderson J, Kernberg O, Michels R, Westen D; Beck; Fonagy; Gabbard; Gunderson; Kernberg; Michels; Westen (September 2010). "Personality Disorders in DSM-5." *American Journal of Psychiatry. 167 (9): 1026–1028.*

Siegel JP (2006). "Dyadic splitting in partner relational disorders." *J Fam Psychol. 20 (3): 418–22.*

Siever, L.J. (1992). "Schizophrenia spectrum disorders." *Review of Psychiatry. 11: 25–42.*

Simonoff E, Elander J, Holmshaw J, Pickles A, Murray R, Rutter M (2004). "Predictors of antisocial personality Continuities from childhood to adult life. *The British Journal of Psychiatry. 184 (2): 118–127.*

Skeem, J. L.; Polaschek, D. L. L.; Patrick, C. J.; Lilienfeld, S. O. (15 December 2011). "Psychopathic Personality: Bridging the Gap Between Scientific Evidence and Public Policy". *Psychological Science in the Public Interest. 12 (3): 95–162.*

Skodol AE, Bender DS (2003). "Why are women diagnosed borderline more than men?". *Psychiatr Q. 74 (4): 349–60.*

Skodol AE; et al. (2002). "Functional Impairment in Patients With Schizotypal, Borderline, Avoidant, or Obsessive–Compulsive Personality Disorder." *Am J Psychiatry. 159: 276–83.*

Slater, A.; Lewis, M. (2006). *Introduction to Infant Development.* Oxford: OUP.

Smith, L. (Ed.) (1992). *Jean Piaget: Critical Assessments* (4 Vols.). London: Routledge.

Smith, L. (Ed.) (1996). *Critical readings on Piaget.* London: Routledge.

Snowden, Ruth (2006). *Teach Yourself Freud.* McGraw-Hill.

Sperry, Len (1995). *Psychopharmacology and Psychotherapy: Strategies for Maximizing Treatment Outcomes.* Psychology Press.

Sperry, Len (2003). "Avoidant Personality Disorder." *Handbook of diagnosis and treatment of DSM-IV-TR personality disorders.* Philadelphia: Brunner-Routledge. pp. 59–79.

Sperry, Lynn (1999). *Narcissistic Personality Disorder, Cognitive Behavior Therapy of DSM-IV Personality*

Disorders: Highly Effective Interventions for the Most Common Personality Disorders. Ann Arbor, MI: Edwards Brothers.

Spiegel, Alix (3 January 2005). "The Dictionary of Disorder: How one man revolutionized psychiatry". *The New Yorker.* Archived from the original on 12 December 2006.

Spiegel, Alix; Glass, Ira (18 January 2002). "81 Words". *This American Life.* Chicago: WBEZ Chicago Public Radio.

Spitzer, Robert L.; Fleiss, Joseph L. (1974). "A re-analysis of the reliability of psychiatric diagnosis". *British Journal of Psychiatry.* 125 (4): 341–347.

Spitzer, R.L. (1981). "The diagnostic status of homosexuality in DSM-III: a reformulation of the issues". *Am J Psychiatry.* 138 (2): 210–215.

Spitzer, First (2005). "Classification of Psychiatric Disorders". *JAMA.* 294 (15): 1898–1899.

Spitzer, Robert L.; Williams, Janet B.W.; First, Michael B.; Gibbon, Miriam. "Biometric Research". *Psychiatric Institute* 2001-2002. New York State Psychiatric Institute. Archived from the original on 7 March 2003.

Spitzer, R.L.; Wakefield, JC. (December 1999). "DSM-IV diagnostic criterion for clinical significance: does it help solve the false positives problem?". *Am J Psychiatry.* 156 (12): 1856–64.

Standing, E.M. (1957). *Maria Montessori: Her Life and Work.* New York: Plume.

Startup, M.; B. Jones; H. Heard; M. Swales; J.M.G. Williams; R.S.P. Jones (November 1999). "Autobiographical memory and dissociation in borderline personality disorder." *Psychological Medicine. 29 (6): 1397–1404.*

Steinberg, Laurence (2008). *Adolescence (8th ed.).* Boston: McGraw-Hill Higher Education.

Steinglass, Joanna (2012). "Increased Capacity to Delay Reward in Anorexia Nervosa." *Journal of the International Neuropsychological Society. 18: 1–8.*

Stern, Adolf (1938). "Psychoanalytic investigation of and therapy in the borderline group of neuroses." *Psychoanalytic Quarterly. 7: 467–489.*

Stevens, Richard (1983). *Erik Erikson: An Introduction.* New York: St. Martin's Press.

Stevens, Richard (2008). *Erik H. Erikson: Explorer of Identity and the Life Cycle.* Basingstoke, England: Palgrave Macmillan.

Stiglmayr CE, Grathwol T, Linehan MM, Ihorst G, Fahrenberg J, Bohus M (May 2005). "Aversive tension in patients with borderline personality disorder: a computer-based controlled field study." *Acta Psychiatr Scand. 111 (5): 372–9.*

Stoffers, JM; Völlm, BA; Rücker, G; Timmer, A; Huband, N; Lieb, K (15 August 2012). "Psychological therapies for people with borderline personality disorder." *The Cochrane database of systematic reviews. 8: CD005652.*

Stone, Michael H. (1993). *Abnormalities of Personality: Within and Beyond the Realm of Treatment.* Norton.

Stone MH (2005). "Borderline Personality Disorder: History of the Concept." In Zanarini MC. *Borderline personality disorder. Boca Raton, FL: Taylor & Francis. pp. 1–18.*

Suinn, Richard M. (1984). *Fundamentals of Abnormal Psychology (Updated ed.).* Chicago: Nelson-Hall.

Sullivan, Harry Stack (1953). *The Interpersonal Theory of Psychiatry.* (N.Y.: W.W. Norton).

"Summary of Practice-Relevant Changes to the DSM-IV-TR". *American Psychiatric Association.* Archived from the original on 13 May 2012.

Sutker, Patricia B., and Albert N. Allain, Jr. (2002). "Antisocial Personality Disorder." Comprehensive Handbook of Psychopathology. Vol. III. : Springer, pp. 445-90.

Sutker, P. B. (2002). *Histrionic, Narcissistic, and Dependent Personality Disorders. Comprehensive handbook of psychopathology (3rd ed.).* New York: Kluwer Academic.

Swartz, Marvin; Blazer, Dan; George, Linda; Winfield, Idee (1990). "Estimating the Prevalence of Borderline Personality Disorder in the Community." *Journal of Personality Disorders. 4 (3): 257–272.*

Szeszko PR, Robinson D, Alvir JM, et al. (October 1999). "Orbital frontal and amygdala volume reductions in obsessive-compulsive disorder." *Arch. Gen. Psychiatry. 56 (10): 913–9.*

Tang YY, Posner MI (Jan 2013). "Special issue on mindfulness neuroscience." *Social Cognitive & Affective Neuroscience. 8 (1): 1–3.*

"TARA Association for Personality Disorder". *tara4bpd.org. Archived from the original on October 20, 2014. Retrieved January 29, 2015.*

Tasca C.; Rapetti M.; Carta M.G.; Fadda B. (2012). "Women and hysteria in the history of mental health." *Clinical Practice & Epidemiology in Mental Health. 8: 110–119.*

Tasman, Allan et al (2008). *Psychiatry. Third Edition.* John Wiley & Sons, Ltd.

Torgersen, S; Lygren, S; Oien, PA; Skre, I; Onstad, S; Edvardsen, J; Tambs, K; Kringlen, E (December 2000). "A twin study of personality disorders." *Comprehensive psychiatry. 41 (6): 416–25.*

Torgersen, S (March 2000). "Genetics of patients with borderline personality disorder." *Psychiatr. Clin. North Am. 23 (1): 1–9.*

Torgersen, S; Lygren, S; Oien, PA; et al. (2000). "A twin study of personality disorders". *Compr Psychiatry. 41 (6): 416–25.*

Trabalzini, Paola (Spring 2011). "Maria Montessori Through the Seasons of the Method". *The NAMTA Journal. 36 (2).*

Upton, Penney (2011). *Developmental Psychology: Critical Thinking in Psychology.* Exeter: Learning Matters.

Urnes, O (30 April 2009). "[Self-harm and personality disorders]." *Tidsskrift for den Norske laegeforening : tidsskrift for praktisk medicin, ny raekke. 129 (9): 872–6.*

Vaillant, George E. (1985). "Maturity of Ego Defenses in Relation to DSM-III Axis II Personality Disorder". *Archives of General Psychiatry. 42 (6): 597.*

Vaillant GE (1992). "The beginning of wisdom is never calling a patient a borderline; or, the clinical management of immature defenses in the treatment of individuals with personality disorders." *J Psychother Pract Res. 1 (2): 117–34.*

Vallacher, R. R. (2017). *Computational Social Psychology.* Routledge.

van Heeringen K, Audenaert K, Van de Wiele L, Verstraete A (November 2000). "Cortisol in violent suicidal behaviour: association with personality and monoaminergic activity." *J Affect Disord. 60 (3): 181–9.*

Van Velzen, C. J. M. (2002). *Social Phobia and Personality Disorders: Comorbidity and Treatment Issues.* Groningen: University Library Groningen.

Vedantam, Shankar (June 26, 2005). "Psychiatry's Missing Diagnosis: Patients' Diversity Is Often Discounted". *The Washington Post.*

Vidal, F. (1994). *Piaget before Piaget.* Cambridge, MA: Harvard University Press.

Villemarette-Pittman, Nicole R; Matthew Stanford; Kevin Greve; Rebecca Houston; Charles Mathias (2004).

"Obsessive-Compulsive Personality Disorder and Behavioral Disinhibition." *The Journal of Psychology. 138 (1): 5–22.*

Wakefield, Jerome C.; PhD, MF; PhD, MB; PhD, DSW; Schmitz, Mark F.; First, Michael B.; MD; Horwitz, Allan V. (2007). "Extending the Bereavement Exclusion for Major Depression to Other Losses: Evidence From the National Comorbidity Survey". *Arch Gen Psychiatry.* 64 (4): 433–440.

Waldinger, Robert J. (1 August 1997). "Psychiatry for Medical Students." *American Psychiatric.*

Walker, E., Kestler, L., Bollini, A.; et al. (2004). "Schizophrenia: etiology and course." *Annual Review of Psychology. 55: 401–430.*

Wallerstein, Robert S.; Goldberger, Leo, eds. (1998). *Ideas and Identities: The Life and Work of Erik Erikson.* Madison, Connecticut: International Universities Press.

Wedding D, Boyd MA, Niemiec RM (2005). *Movies and Mental Illness: Using Films to Understand Psychopathology.* Cambridge, MA: Hogrefe.

Weiner, M. B. (1979). "Caring for the Elderly. Psychological Aging: Aspects of Normal Personality and Development in Old Age. Part II. Erik Erikson: Resolutions of Psychosocial Tasks". *The Journal of Nursing Care. 12 (5): 27–28.*

Welchman, Kit (2000). *Erik Erikson: His Life, Work, and Significance.* Buckingham, England: Open University Press.

West, Malcolm L. and A. E. Sheldon-Keller (1994). *Patterns of Relating An Adult Attachment Perspective.* New York: Guilford Press.

Widiger, T. (1998). "Sex biases in the diagnosis of personality disorders." *Journal of Personality Disorders. 12 (2): 95–118.*

Widiger TA, Sankis LM (2000). "Adult psychopathology: issues and controversies". *Annu Rev Psychol.* 51 (1): 377–404.

Wilson, M. (March 1993). "DSM-III and the transformation of American psychiatry: a history". *Am J Psychiatry.* 150 (3): 399–410.

Wing, Peter C. (1997). "Patient or Client? If in Doubt, Ask." *Canadian Medical Association, 157:287-89.*

Winnicott, Donald (1965): *The Maturational Process and the Facilitating Environment.* Karnac Books.
Winnicott, Donald (2006). *The Family and Individual Development.* Routledge.

Winnicott, Donald (2012). *Playing and Reality.* Routledge Classics.

Wolff, Sula (1995). *Loners - The Life Path of Unusual Children.* Routledge.

Wood, S.E.; Wood, C.E.; Boyd D. (2006). *Mastering the world of psychology (2 ed.).* Allyn & Bacon.

Woodbury-Smith, MR and F. R. Volkmar (2008). "Asperger syndrome." *Eur Child Adolesc Psychiatry. 18 (1): 2–11.*

Yamagata-Lynch, L.C (2010). *Activity Systems Analysis Methods: Understanding Complex Learning Environments.* New York, NY: Springer Science.

Yang, Yaling; Raine, Adrian (30 November 2009). "Prefrontal Structural and Functional Brain Imaging findings in Antisocial, Violent, and Psychopathic Individuals: A Meta-Analysis." *Psychiatry Research. 174 (2): 81–88.*

Yildirim, Bariş O. (August 2013). "Systematic review, structural analysis, and new theoretical perspectives on the role of serotonin and associated genes in the etiology of psychopathy and sociopathy." *Neuroscience & Biobehavioral Reviews. 37: 1254–1296.*

Zanarini, MC; Frankenburg, FR (1997). "Pathways to the development of borderline personality disorder." *J. Pers. Disord.* 11 (1): 93–104.

Zanarini MC, Frankenburg FR, DeLuca CJ, Hennen J, Khera GS, Gunderson JG (1998). "The pain of being borderline: dysphoric states specific to borderline personality disorder." *Harv Rev Psychiatry. 6 (4): 201–7.*

Zanarini MC, Frankenburg FR, Dubo ED, et al. (December 1998). "Axis I comorbidity of borderline personality disorder." *Am J Psychiatry. 155 (12): 1733–9.*

Zanarini MC, Frankenburg FR, Reich DB, et al. (2000). "Biparental failure in the childhood experiences of borderline patients." *J Personal Disord. 14 (3): 264–73.*

Zanarini MC, Frankenburg FR, Khera GS, Bleichmar J (2001). "Treatment histories of borderline inpatients." *Compr Psychiatry. 42 (2): 144–50.*

The Learning Spectrum

About the Author

John H. Morgan, Ph.D.(Hartford), D.Sc.(London), Psy.D. (Foundation House/Oxford) is Research Professor of Clinical Psychopathology (GTF/Indiana) and is currently the Editor-in-Chief of *The Behavioral Mind: A Journal of Personality Disorders* published by MacBain & Boyd. Until his recent retirement, he was Senior Fellow in Behavioral Sciences of Foundation House/Oxford (UK) where he taught a doctoral-level seminar and served as a member of the Board of Studies for twenty years in the international summer program of Oxford University (UK). Dr. Morgan has held postdoctoral appointments to Harvard, Yale, and Princeton and is a former National Science Foundation Science Faculty Fellow at the University of Notre Dame. He has also held three appointments as a Postdoctoral Research Scholar at the University of Chicago. In 2010, he was a Visiting Scholar at New York University and in 2015 was appointed Visiting Scholar at Harvard University for the third time in his academic career. The author/editor of over 30 books, his latest book is *Child Psychopathology in Clinical Practice: The Psychoanalytic Theories of Karen Horney, Melanie Klein, and Anna Freud (2019)*. In the field of psychopathology, he has recently published a three-volume series titled *Psychopathology: Clinical Studies in Personality Disorders; Clinical Psychotherapy: A History of Theory and Practice;* and *Understanding Ourselves: Essays in the History and Philosophy of the Social Sciences.* A major contribution to the research community in the area of clinical psychotherapy is his 2019 reference work *An Encyclopedic Dictionary of Interpersonal Psychotherapy: Concepts and Terms* published by MacBain & Boyd. Dr. Morgan holds professional memberships in the American Psychological

Association, the Society of Clinical Psychology, and the Society of Behavioral Medicine and is an elected member of the American Psychopathological Association.   He is currently under contract for the writing of *Psychoanalysis: The Comprehensive Reference Dictionary (based on the Standard Edition of the Collected Psychological Works of Sigmund Freud).*

www.ingramcontent.com/pod-product-compliance
Lightning Source LLC
Chambersburg PA
CBHW050650270326
41927CB00012B/2953